just plain smart ™

personal
finance
advisor

H&R Block just plain smart™ Personal Finance Advisor

H&R BLOCK

just plain smart™

personal finance advisor

A lifelong
approach to achieving your financial goals

RANDOM HOUSE
REFERENCE
NEW YORK

table of contents with selected topics

introduction

M any of us ignore our personal finances and therefore miss extraordinary opportunities. Why? Maybe it's because dealing with personal finances can seem complicated and overwhelming. Maybe it's because it's easier to delay making serious financial decisions or ignore financial matters altogether. While it can certainly be more fun to spend money than to stick to a plan to save it—you'll be glad you did when you begin to achieve your financial goals.

Understanding your personal finances takes time and effort. But if you want to exercise more control over your financial future, you need to plan ahead. The first step in creating a sound personal financial plan is to believe that you can do it. Once you have the *confidence* that you can create a financial plan that works, the next step is to acquire the right *financial information*. Then, the *process* becomes important—committing to the process of change. Probably the most important part of a sound personal financial plan is what we call the *accountability factor*. Are you starting to improve your financial situation? Are you achieving your goals? It is important to periodically monitor your progress.

By incorporating the four steps mentioned above—confidence, information, process, and accountability—you will be well on the way to achieving your financial dreams. There's no reason why you can't manage your money well enough to enjoy both a prosperous work life and a comfortable retirement. You need a well-conceived personal financial blueprint and the discipline to use it.

The **H&R Block Personal Finance Advisor,** one of several books in the H&R Block just plain smart™ Advisor Series of reliable tax and financial guides, will not only help you learn about personal finances, but also help you develop a financial blueprint and help prepare you for opportunities and challenges as they present themselves. Whenever possible, you can plan ahead to meet major financial challenges and take full advantage by making more informed decisions along the way. Because taxes touch upon and affect all aspects of personal finance, H&R Block, the world's largest tax services company, has the experience to understand your financial goals and the expertise to help you achieve them. Use the H&R Block just plain smart™ Advisor Series to put our experience to work for you.

How to Use This Book

The **Personal Finance Advisor** is designed to help you exercise more control over your personal finances. It covers a wide variety of topics from budgeting, saving, and investing to planning for college, retirement, and your estate. The book features dozens of worksheets and sidebars—useful "fast facts," action-packed "smart steps," and clear "plain talk" definitions. It also contains scenarios derived from real-life situations. This guide should arm you with the knowledge you need to understand your personal financial situation, to plan ahead, and to achieve your financial goals.

We've organized the **Personal Finance Advisor** as a step-by-step resource with helpful tools necessary to guide you through your financial life. Keep it handy and consult it throughout the year as certain events occur (such as purchasing insurance, buying a home, or changing jobs). You'll be able to make informed decisions and adjustments as your personal situation changes.

Online Learning Resources

An important part of the process of achieving your financial goals is to actually get started. Throughout the book, you'll find numerous "online" Smart Steps that will enable you to immediately put into practice (via the Internet) some of the topics that have just been covered. In addition, you"ll gain access to a variety of inter-active tools and calculators that will help you make the most of the **Personal Finance Advisor.** Don't delay—start now.

Start Now!

Use online learning resources to get started today.

Log on to
hrblock.com/advisor

Look for the Web site address hrblock.com/advisor inside of the Smart Steps (pictured at left), log on, and get started today!

What's the Next Step?

Decide how much of the **Personal Finance Advisor** applies to you and choose what steps to take. Turn to it when you make or modify your plans. It will help you ask informed questions of your professional advisors. Whether you do it all on your own or work with the help of financial professionals, you'll be better equipped to handle your personal finances wisely.

Acknowledgments

While it is not possible to list everyone who made the **H&R Block Personal Finance Advisor** possible, we would like to acknowledge the following organizations and individuals for their many contributions to this book: **The College for Financial Planning** ▪ **Random House Reference** ▪ **RSM McGladrey, Inc.** ▪ **and the many dedicated associates and tax and financial professionals of H&R Block.**

H&R Block

1 [PERSONAL FINANCE 101:

Why It Pays to Plan Your Finances]

"A goal without a plan is only a wish."

—Hal Becker

Personal financial planning involves managing your finances properly to meet your life goals. You determine where you are financially, where you want to be in the future, and what you need to do to get there—how to get from point A to point B. But if you're going to put in the effort, you may as well reap the rewards. It takes some organization and a common-sense financial blueprint to reach reasonable financial goals. It can also be helpful to consult with a financial advisor once you develop a financial blueprint so you can then develop a formal financial plan.

Regardless of how complex your financial situation is, you *can* begin successfully managing your finances and meeting your goals once you're armed with the tools and techniques described in this book. Whether it is going on a nice vacation, buying a second family vehicle, sending your kids to college, enjoying a comfortable retirement, or buying a first or second home, you can achieve your financial dreams with persistence and a well-rooted savings mentality.

Let's get started!

Where to Start

The first step toward an effective personal financial plan is organization. You need to know your spending patterns—when, where, and how you have been spending your money. Then you need to determine some spending and savings priorities. Decide which of your ongoing expenses are the most important to you, and which are the least important. Until you identify your spending habits and priorities, you won't be able to make the spending cuts you need, get out of debt, fund a savings, investment or retirement plan, or meet your other financial goals.

Get organized by gathering your important financial documents and filing them in one convenient location. Many people have their bills, receipts, and financial documents scattered in drawers, boxes, and closets from one end of the house to the other. Maybe you've stored some of the information in the garage, or even in your desk at work. Gather it all, not just the papers you save for tax preparation time.

Tools for Setting Up a Basic Filing System

The first step in record keeping is to acquire:

- **A filing cabinet or desk drawer to store your records**
- **File folders**
- **Labels to tag the folders**
- **A pen or marker**
  and/or
- **A reliable computer, your favorite financial spreadsheet or software, and disks or CD-ROMs for making back-ups of your files for electronic record keeping**

As the old cliché asks, "How can you know where you're going if you don't know where you are?" Only by gathering your financial records will you be able to identify your income and expenses. If you don't have enough records to determine your expenses—such as how much you spend on entertainment and clothes—you may have to track how you spend money over a few months. You won't be able to plan and make changes in your spending habits unless you know what your income and expenses are. Not knowing is like aiming at a target while you're blindfolded.

smart step

Make sure that your spouse or partner agrees with the record-keeping system, and decide who's going to be the main keeper of the records.

What to Keep

Here's a list that can help you decide exactly what to do with those piles of paper.

Legal Documents—Any documents that deal with major life events, such as birth, death, or marriage, should be kept for a lifetime, in a safe and secure location. Documents in this category include:

- **Adoption papers**
- **Birth certificates**
- **Business ownership papers**
- **Citizenship papers and passports**
- **Contracts for funeral arrangements and cemetery plots**
- **Death certificates**
- **Deeds and titles**
- **Divorce-related documents**
- **Education records**
- **Home purchase contracts**
- **Insurance policies**
- **Last wills and testaments**
- **Living wills**
- **Loan documents**
- **Marriage certificates**
- **Military service records**
- **Powers of attorney**
- **Social Security cards**
- **Trust documents**

When finding a place to store documents that your family or executor will need when you die or become incapacitated (such as your will and power of attorney), make sure that the appropriate person has easy access to the records. A safe deposit box may seem like a good place to keep those documents, but it may not be. In some states, your safe deposit box would remain sealed until the estate goes through **probate**. If your will is in that box, it could delay the process significantly.

Tax Records—Tax returns should be kept at least six years in a reasonably secure place. Three years is generally the limit for the IRS to audit your return, but if they question something substantial, they can also check the previous three years in some instances. If they suspect fraud, they can probe even further.

How long you keep supporting documentation such as checking account statements or receipts may depend on how easily they can be replaced. For example, there's little point in keeping things such as pay stubs, household bills, or quarterly mutual fund statements more than a year or so. Canceled checks should probably be kept for at least three years, and you might hold on to W-2 forms indefinitely.

Receipts that show what you paid for big-ticket items such as jewelry or items in a collection can help if you later need to file an insurance claim on the items or to determine your gain or loss for tax purposes if you sell them.

Investment Records—Statements that show what you've bought or sold and for how much, and what your investments have earned should be kept until six years after you sell the investment and have paid any tax on the gain or have finished deducting any loss. Keep retirement plan records at least until you have withdrawn all the money from the account.

Financial Documents—How long you keep insurance policies depends on what type they are. Life insurance policies should be kept for the life of the policy (make sure your heirs have easy access); health and disability policies should be kept for as long as they're applicable. Property insurance policies such as home-

plain talk

Probate is the state's legal procedure for verifying that a will is authentic and administering the settlement of the estate.

smart step

Set a deadline for gathering the records and documents you need to develop your financial blueprint. Instead of sorting your papers again and again, try to set up the record-keeping system you'll use for life.

owners, rental, and auto insurance can usually be discarded a year or two after they expire. Keep any employee benefit statements for a year or two as well.

If you've made loans to others, keep the documentation until the loans are paid in full. Documents showing you've paid a loan in full should be kept permanently in case there's ever any question about whether you still owe money.

Documents Checklist

Here's a checklist of documents and records that you'll need to find for your new and improved record-keeping system.

✓ Document/Record	Location
☐ Adoption papers	_____
☐ Birth and death certificates	_____
☐ Business agreements	_____
☐ Cemetery plots	_____
☐ Citizenship papers/passports	_____
☐ Deeds and titles	_____
☐ Divorce papers	_____
☐ Insurance policies	_____
☐ Investment papers	_____
☐ Marriage certificates	_____
☐ Pension/retirement plans	_____
☐ Powers of attorney	_____
☐ Rental leases/mortgage papers	_____
☐ School transcripts	_____
☐ Tax returns and records	_____
☐ Will and trust documents	_____

Once you're organized, make preparations in case disaster strikes. In a notebook or computer file, record key information about where to find your safe deposit box (or wherever you store your important documents), bank and brokerage accounts, insurance policies, tax records, deeds, and anything else your family or heirs might need. This file will be your master document locator. In Chapter 2, we'll suggest a format for recording important personal information in one document. Make sure that both the master document locator and the listing of personal information are easy to find because they are critical to your financial blueprint.

Where Do You Want to Go?

When you take a trip, it helps to have a destination in mind. Otherwise, you'll never get there. The same is true with your personal finances. Once you've gotten your paperwork organized, you can begin deciding what you'd like your money to do for you. What do you want out of life, for yourself, for your family, for your future?

- **A new home?**
- **A college education for your child?**
- **A comfortable retirement?**
- **A nice car?**
- **A vacation home?**

Only after you set your goals can you take steps to achieve them. Write everything down—all your hopes, dreams, and material aspirations—and don't be afraid to dream big. Be specific about your goals. For example, "retire early" is a good start, but "retire at age fifty-five with $500,000 in savings" is better. "Buy a three-bedroom home in five years" is better than "have a nice home."

smart step

Check with your attorney to learn what laws are applicable in your state when deciding which documents to keep in your safe deposit box.

Maintain a
complete, up-
to-date infor-
mation list of
the location of
your important
records and
documents.
Tell key people
such as your
spouse, an adult
child, or your
lawyer where
these papers
are kept.

Later in this chapter, you'll have the chance to write down your short-term, intermediate, and long-term goals.

Give yourself some motivation to put together a sound financial plan that will work for you. Knowing exactly what you want can help you make the sacrifices—cutting back on expenses for unnecessary items or working a second job—much easier to handle. When you keep the big picture in mind, it's easier to resist the daily temptations that can ruin your budget.

When putting together your financial goals, don't get caught up in the details. Your goals, over time, are likely to change. Suddenly, maternity blouses may seem more important than a new sequined dinner dress, and that flashy convertible you wanted might not accommodate a baby seat. You can always adjust your goals. It's a living document—a work in progress. But without a destination in mind, you may never leave the driveway.

Where Do You Stand Now?

Now that you can visualize your castles in the sky, the next step is to figure out how you're going to achieve those dreams. The best way to start is to figure out where you stand now. To help you identify your income and spending patterns, as well as your current assets and liabilities, we've included two important worksheets: the Cash Flow Worksheet and the Net Worth Worksheet.

To complete the Cash Flow Worksheet (shown on page 10), you'll first write down everything you currently earn monthly from your job, your investments, and any other type of income you receive on a regular basis, such as rental income, disability or veterans' benefits, trust fund income, etc. This part of the worksheet represents your monthly income from all sources. Naturally, you'll include your spouse's sources of income if you're married.

In addition, write down everything you spend on a monthly basis. We've provided a list of expenses to get you started. Some of the categories may not apply to you, and you may have some expenses not listed on the worksheet. For example, you may be paying alimony or child support. If so, you can write them on the "Other" line. (Of course, if you were on the receiving end of such payments, you would list them as income.)

Not all expenses are paid monthly. If you make payments once a year, such as insurance premiums or real estate taxes, you can divide the amount by twelve and list one month's worth on your budget. This way you won't take a big hit in one month on your budget.

Once you subtract your expenses from your income, you hopefully have something left over. If you don't, you'll need to take a close look at your expenses to see what you can eliminate, or at least reduce. Or you can figure out how to increase your income. These funds can be used for any purpose, such as additional savings, reducing debt, charitable giving, or even additional purchases—and are often referred to as **discretionary income**.

plain talk

Discretionary income is money left over after you have paid all your expenses, including taxes. This "leftover" income is what you earmark for achieving your financial goals.

Your Financial Blueprint

Try to include all relevant information on the Cash Flow Worksheet. In order to do the job correctly, you may need to examine credit card statements, checkbooks, utility bills, mortgage or rent payments, store receipts, and ATM slips.

CASH FLOW WORKSHEET

MONTHLY INCOME

Alimony/child support	_____
Investment income	_____
Salary/wages	$ _____
Self-employment income	_____
Other income	_____
Total monthly income	$ _____

MONTHLY EXPENSES

Automobile	$ _____
Charitable contributions	_____
Child care	_____
Clothing	_____
Dues/subscriptions	_____
Education	_____
Entertainment	_____
Food	_____
Gifts	_____
Home maintenance	_____
Insurance	_____
Investments	_____
Loans	_____
Medical/dental	_____
Mortgage/rent	_____
Retirement	_____
Savings	_____
Taxes	_____
Transportation	_____
Utilities	_____
Vacation	_____
Other	_____
Total monthly expenses	$ _____

Monthly income	$ _____
− Monthly expenses	_____
= Monthly discretionary income	$ _____

Don't skip the worksheet because you're afraid you might not include every detail. Just do the best you can. You can revise it later. The key is to get something in writing to help you begin your personal financial blueprint. It's important to be honest. Only if you see the true picture can you take the action you need to minimize your spending and maximize your savings.

In addition to completing the Cash Flow Worksheet, you might find it useful (and even necessary) to maintain a spending diary for a few months. Write down every dollar you spend—on meals, groceries, clothing, entertainment, automotive expenses, vacations, and all other purchases and expenses. This activity should help you nail down some expenses that you only guessed at when you completed the Cash Flow Worksheet.

In fact, you might find vast discrepancies between the expenses you write down on the worksheet—the money you think you spend—with the amounts you enter in your diary—the money you actually spend. Only by identifying exactly where you spend your money can you take the appropriate action to adjust your spending habits to accommodate a more generous savings program.

Finally, when you know how you actually spend your money, you can develop a budget. And only with a budget in place can you track where your money goes. User-friendly software is available to track your income, your expenses, as well as your assets and liabilities. Remember, setting up a budget is not a negative! It's a very positive action. You can always choose to spend more money than your budget *allows*, but at least you'll be aware that you have chosen to do so. And setting up a budget doesn't mean you're depriving yourself. It means you're planning to reach your goals. (For more information on budgets, see Chapter 2.)

smart step

Keep a spending diary for a few months. You'll develop an accurate picture of how your money is being spent and will be able to identify some places to cut back if necessary.

Your Financial Snapshot

Your net worth is the amount of money you would have if you sold everything you own at fair market value and paid off all your debts.

Where do you want to be financially in five years, ten years, and during your retirement? What are your family's financial goals? How much will you need to save each month to reach those goals? Throughout this book, we will help you determine how much you will need to save and invest to pursue your financial goals.

The following Goals Worksheets will get you started. We have organized the worksheets into three time frames for you:

1. **Short-term goals** such as establishing an emergency fund, adequate insurance coverage, and items that will be purchased on an annual basis (goals for the next six to twelve months)
2. **Intermediate-term goals** such as a new car or home (goals for the next year or two)
3. **Long-term goals** such as starting a new business (goals for the next three to five years)

By filling out the Net Worth Worksheet, you can get a snapshot of your financial situation. Think of it as a measure of your financial health. List the value of everything you own (assets). Then list the amounts you owe (liabilities). The difference is your **net worth**, and this is the amount you want to see increasing over time. By knowing your current net worth, you can set a net worth goal for next year. And for the year after that!

The asset category on the following worksheet is further divided into three categories: liquid assets, investment assets, and personal assets. When valuing assets, enter the amount you could currently receive if you sold them, not the amount you paid, which could be more or less than current market value.

NET WORTH WORKSHEET

LIQUID ASSETS

Cash and checking accounts	$ _____
CDs	_____
Credit union accounts	_____
Money market accounts	_____
Savings accounts	_____
Other	_____
Total Liquid Assets	$ _____

INVESTMENT ASSETS

Annuities	$ _____
Bonds	_____
Business interests	_____
Education accounts	_____
Mutual funds	_____
Real estate (other than your home)	_____
Retirement accounts	_____
Stocks	_____
Other	_____
Total Investment Assets	$ _____

PERSONAL ASSETS

Appliances/computers	$ _____
Automobiles/boats	_____
Furnishings	_____
Jewelry/art	_____
Residence	_____
Vacation home	_____
Other	_____
Total Personal Assets	$ _____
Grand Total of Assets	$ _____

LIABILITIES

Auto loans	$ _____
Bank loans	_____
Credit card balances	_____
Education loans	_____
Home mortgage	_____
Other mortgage	_____
Personal loans	_____
Other	_____
Total Liabilities	$ _____

Total Assets	$ _____
– Total Liabilities	_____
= Your Net Worth	$ _____

List your primary goals and attach a time frame in years and assign a dollar amount to each goal in the following worksheets.

SHORT-TERM GOALS WORKSHEET (6–12 months)

GOAL	TIME FRAME	$ AMOUNT NEEDED
▪ Buy/lease a car	_____	_____
▪ Charitable contributions	_____	_____
▪ Emergency fund	_____	_____
▪ Home improvements	_____	_____
▪ Insurance purchases	_____	_____
Automobile	_____	_____
Disability	_____	_____
Health	_____	_____
Homeowners or renters	_____	_____
Life	_____	_____
Long-term care	_____	_____
Other	_____	_____
▪ Pay off debt	_____	_____
Automobile	_____	_____
Bills	_____	_____
Credit cards	_____	_____
▪ Other funds	_____	_____
Automobile	_____	_____
Clothes	_____	_____
Entertainment	_____	_____
Gifts	_____	_____
Health	_____	_____
Vacation	_____	_____
Other	_____	_____

INTERMEDIATE-TERM GOALS WORKSHEET (1–2 years)

GOAL	TIME FRAME	$ AMOUNT NEEDED
Buy/own a home	_____	_____
Education fund	_____	_____
Investment plan	_____	_____
Other funds	_____	_____
Automobile	_____	_____
Clothes	_____	_____
Entertainment	_____	_____
Gifts	_____	_____
Health	_____	_____
Vacation	_____	_____
Other	_____	_____

LONG-TERM GOALS WORKSHEET (3–5 years)

GOAL	TIME FRAME	$ AMOUNT NEEDED
Investment plan	_____	_____
Pay off mortgage	_____	_____
Retirement plan	_____	_____
Start new business	_____	_____
Vacation home	_____	_____
Other	_____	_____

smart step

Start Now!

Create your Net Worth Worksheet and set your goals.

Log on to
hrblock.com/advisor

Once you have set specific goals for saving, putting the money away can be easy. In fact, many financial institutions offer you the option of having a set amount of money withdrawn from your checking account each month for deposit into an investment or savings plan. No checks to write, no action to take—you don't need to give it a thought. Your money is automatically transferred into a savings or investment plan for you. In a sense, you pay yourself first.

THE CHALLENGE

Vicki and Andy are in their mid-twenties and have been married a couple of years. With no kids and two incomes, they wanted to save for a home and for the arrival of children in the next few years. However, each month they were just breaking even, and had begun making only the minimum payments on their credit card bills when money was especially tight. "We weren't exactly in trouble financially, but we weren't getting ahead, either," Vicki explained.

THE PLAN

Vicki and Andy sat down one Saturday to discuss their finances. They determined that their monthly income, after taxes, was about $3,000. They then examined their monthly expenses. By their best estimate, they were spending about $2,500 each month, leaving, theoretically, $500 for their savings. But, where was the money? "That $500 was doing a disappearing act that would make a magician proud," Andy said.

As the next part of their plan, Vicki and Andy agreed to write down every cent they spent for the next month. "Was that ever an eye-opener!" exclaimed Vicki. Among the things they discovered is that they were dining out about two evenings a week, something they both enjoy. The average tab for an evening out? $50, or about $400 per month. They also learned that they both went out to lunch every workday, at a daily average cost of $7. That comes to about $300 per month. Also during the month, three magazine subscriptions came due. One magazine they read faithfully, but the other two gathered dust.

Vicki and Andy decided they needed to reduce the amount of money they were spending at restaurants. They agreed to go out to dinner just once a week, and they would alternate choosing the place. They also agreed to pack their lunches three days a week and go out to lunch with co-workers the other two days. And they canceled the subscriptions for the magazines they didn't read. All the money they saved they agreed to put into a bank account until there was enough there to consider other investment options. "We're still not saving as much as we would like," said Andy, "but we're both due for raises soon, and we're determined to add that money to our savings."

Did You Know That. . .?

You don't need to know everything about how the financial world works, but you do need to know some basics as they apply to your personal finances. Here are a few pieces of information that will help make you a savvy financial citizen:

smart step

➤ Did You Know That . . .

- **A master document locator is fundamental to effective financial planning?** See Chapter 2 for ways to get your financial papers organized so you can set goals and start working on your financial blueprint.
- **You may be able to simplify your financial life and save time and money if you do your banking transactions online?** Chapter 3 includes information on online banking as an alternative to bricks-and-mortar banking.
- **You may qualify to have part of your student loans canceled if you work in a certain job?** See Chapter 4 to learn how you can build and maintain good credit and how to manage debt better.
- **If you start saving $1,000 annually at the beginning of each year starting at age thirty, you would have over $140,000 accumulated at age sixty-five, assuming an annual return of 7 percent and no withdrawals?** See Chapter 5 for tips on cutting expenses and saving more toward your goals.
- **You need to insure all your major assets, including your ability to earn a living?** See Chapter 6 for help understanding how different types of insurance work, what to insure, and the amounts of insurance you need.
- **You are allowed to drop private mortgage insurance (PMI) when you have built up 20 percent of the home's value as equity?** See Chapter 7 for help with financing a home purchase.
- **Through diversification and asset allocation, you can manage investment risks under various economic conditions?** See Chapter 8 to learn about the basics of investing, including risk and reward and matching various types of investments to your needs and level of risk tolerance.

When you get your annual raise from your job, consider increasing your automatic savings or investment plan by a similar amount.

- **Most states have plans that allow you to save money for your child's college education and many states offer excellent tax benefits?** Chapter 9 will show how your child can go to college without forcing you to go too far into debt.

- **You can borrow from a 401(k) plan but not from an IRA account?** See Chapter 10 for a wealth of information about achieving a financially secure retirement.

- **An emergency fund equal to three to six months' expenses is the best way to keep your finances on track when the unexpected happens?** See Chapter 11 to discover helpful strategies for dealing with unplanned situations such as losing your job, getting divorced, falling ill, or receiving an unexpected windfall.

- **If you don't plan ahead, the state will decide for you how your assets will be distributed?** Chapter 12 will describe why you need a will and a variety of ways you can pass assets on to your heirs and to charity while minimizing estate taxes.

Some people are adequately equipped with the tools they need to develop attainable goals. But a majority of us first have to educate ourselves about personal financial planning and then rely on financial professionals to help us develop a financial plan. Reading the **Personal Finance Advisor** will help provide you with the knowledge to create a financial blueprint and help you to be better informed when you work with a professional financial advisor.

the ESSENTIALS

1 Organize by gathering your important financial papers and filing them in one convenient location.

2 Make sure you have a record of what's where, especially items your family and heirs will need immediately after your death.

3 The first step in getting a handle on your finances is knowing how your money is being spent and where you would like it to go.

4 Set your goals. Although some financial goals can change, without a destination in mind, you'll never get started on the journey.

5 Figure out what works, what will get you closer to your goals, and do more of it.

2 [MONEY SMARTS:
Developing a Financial Blueprint]

"Today's preparation determines tomorrow's achievement."
—Anonymous

You'll need to
determine the
desired end
result before
you begin to
map the finan-
cial route you
will take to get
there.

Financial planning can be a fulfilling experience. It gives you the chance to organize your affairs, determine your financial fitness, adopt spending priorities, set some savings and investment goals, and chart a course to reach those goals. Putting together a personal financial plan could be one of the most important activities of your life.

Financial planning can do more than just improve your fiscal health—it could also improve your physical health. You'll probably sleep better knowing where you stand financially, where you're going, and how you're going to get there.

Financial planning is not something you do once and then forget about. As your life changes, your financial circumstances will also change, and that often means adjusting your blueprint. But you still need a basic plan to get you started. Think of a financial plan as your personal global positioning system. You tell it where you want to go, and it suggests the best routes and guides you along the way. It even helps adjust the directions if circumstances change. But over the long haul, your plan will help guide you to your financial destination.

There are six elements of personal financial planning that will help guide you to financial freedom.

1. Determine your current financial situation and develop a budget and process to manage debt.
2. Determine the adequate amount of insurance coverage on your life, and for your disability, long-term care, and property needs.
3. Develop specific goals and start saving for them.
4. Utilize employer retirement plans and IRAs to accumulate wealth for retirement.
5. Review your income tax planning to minimize the effects of taxes on your income and investments.
6. Execute a will and other estate documents to pass your assets on the way you want.

The Personal Finance Advisor touches on all of these elements, and the illustration below emphasizes how they work together in contributing to your financial well-being.

Elements of
Financial Planning

Source: H&R Block

There are many
myths surround-
ing financial
planning. Being
informed can
help you sepa-
rate myth from
reality.

Financial Planning Myths

Many people put off financial planning because of misconceptions about the process. Here are some common myths about financial planning.

Myth: I don't have the time to do it.

Reality: Free time is something that seems to shrink rather than expand as the years go by. You will probably never have "more time." You need to *make* time for financial planning. But that may not be as difficult as it seems. If you have time to visit with friends and watch television, you can certainly find some time to work on your financial plan.

Myth: Why would I need a financial plan when I have no money?

Reality: A lack of financial planning may be one reason you have no money. The whole point of financial planning is to help you improve your financial condition. Financial planning can help put money back in your pocket.

Myth: I can't afford a financial advisor.

Reality: There are many options available to you. Many financial advisors are interested in having you for a client with the expectation that they will be able to assist you in the future as your income rises and your planning needs increase.

Myth: I don't know enough about investing and financial planning.

Reality: Everyone enters the investment world as a beginner. Even legendary stock market billionaire Warren Buffett was once a new investor who had to learn the ropes. This book will teach you the basics. But to really learn to succeed as an investor, you need to dive in, learn enough to make that first investment, and then continue to learn as you go. The sooner you start, the more experience you'll gain, which should help you to be more successful over the long run.

Myth: I can't even pay my bills. How am I going to follow a financial plan?

Reality: If you're already having financial difficulty, you're the perfect candidate for financial planning. By sitting down and working out a sound financial plan, you may be able to figure out a way to get out from under your bills, keep your bills from piling up, and start planning for your future needs.

Myth: Why make a plan? I won't stick to it anyway.

Reality: Money can be a motivating factor. When you see how much wealth you can accumulate through a common-sense financial plan, you may be more motivated to stick with it.

Myth: I have a plan. I just have it in my head.

Reality: If it isn't written down, it isn't a plan. Besides, there are some important aspects of financial planning that you can't keep in your head—such as your will and other estate planning documents. Your financial picture will become clearer in terms of where you stand, where you want to go, and how you're going to get there once you have a plan in writing.

**smart
step**

If you're split-
ting expenses
with someone,
you may want
to keep your
finances sepa-
rate. It could
save you some
big headaches
if the two of
you part ways
later.

Managing Your Finances

Individuals are often worlds apart in the way they view money and investing. Some married couples and other people who share income and expenses sometimes fight about money. One may have the saving habit, and the other may spend money as quickly as it's earned—or even before!

How can you resolve those differences? First, you start by talking. You'll proba-bly find that the solution to many of your conflicts will become clearer when you look objectively at your financial situation and the steps needed to reach your long-term goals. Here's what is involved:

■ **Determine your most important financial goals by using the work-sheets in Chapter 1.** This may require some compromises, but try to at least agree on the major items, such as staying current with your bills, saving for a home, a retirement nest egg, or college for the children.
■ **Calculate how much you will need to save and invest each month to reach those goals.**
■ **Add your joint monthly income and expenditures.** (Use the Cash Flow Worksheet in Chapter 1.)
■ **Make the parts fit—the amount you make, the amount you spend, and the amount you need to save.** That may mean trimming some expenditures to come up with enough money to meet your monthly savings goals or finding a way to generate additional income—and it may also require a willingness to compromise. To make a budget work for the long-term good of the household finances, both partners may have to sacrifice.

We'll discuss how to create a budget in the next section.

By reviewing your financial matters now and agreeing on a plan of action, you can avoid a financial crisis later that could jeopardize both your financial well-being and your partnership.

The toughest areas of agreement tend to be the budget—deciding which expenses have top priority and which have to go—and the investment approach. One partner may want a high-risk portfolio with the greatest potential for gain, while the other may prefer to keep all the money in an insured bank account. Compromise will no doubt be in order here. You need to agree on a diversified portfolio that provides an adequate degree of safety along with the potential for an adequate return on investment. (For more on investing, see Chapter 8.)

If you can't reconcile your differences, or if you're unable to get your partner on board with the financial planning process, you may need outside help. Financial planners and investment advisors are trained to help you put together a lifetime savings and investment program that both parties can live with.

Creating Your Budget

Be proud of yourself! If you followed the advice in Chapter 1, you've gathered all your important financial records and documents, determined where you stand (by completing the Cash Flow Worksheet and the Net Worth Worksheet), and written down your financial goals. You're on your way to financial health.

It's time to create a budget. Yes, a budget! Think of it as a spending plan. You may have to modify it, and that's okay. Give your spending plan a chance to work. If you stick to it, you can reach your goals.

Now's the time to think about those daily expenses that can be controlled, such as gourmet coffee in the morning and lunch at restaurants near the office. You'll need to evaluate the expenses you can control and set some guidelines to increase your discretionary income. This book includes all sorts of tips to help you decrease your expenses, even those you might consider fixed, such as transportation and mortgage payments.

The first step is to review the Goals Worksheets you developed in Chapter 1. What you need to do now is determine how much you can put aside each month to accumulate the amount you listed in the worksheets. For example, let's say one of your goals is to build an adequate emergency fund. You already have some savings earmarked for this in a money market fund, but you want to save another $5,000. Assume also that you want to have the emergency fund in place within twenty-four months. In Chapter 5, you'll learn about the magic of compounding and the time value of money. But for now, let's assume that you would need to save approximately $185 monthly.

Build this monthly savings amount into the expenses portion of your budget. Remember, you want to pay yourself first—well, at least after you pay the mortgage, utilities, food, etc. If you plan to save, you won't need to depend on something being left over after you subtract expenditures from income.

Now that you see the importance of including savings *in* your budget, here are several key steps to take:

Draw Up a Spending Blueprint—A well-conceived spending blueprint can help you keep your expenditures in check. You may find that you need to cut back in some areas in order to afford the things that are most important to you. For example, you may decide to set an amount for entertainment (concerts, movies, dining out, video rentals) and stick to it—rather than eating out on a whim and being the first on the block to see the current hit at the cineplex.

Focus on Long-Term Goals—It's much easier to pass on the unnecessary expenses when you've made the decision to buy a home in four or five years. Setting big goals can be a powerful savings incentive.

Make Saving Automatic—Pay yourself first by using payroll deduction or automatic investing programs.

Monitor Your Progress—Every six months or so, check to see if you're meeting your financial goals. If you're behind schedule, you may need to make some other cuts or find ways to increase income. But if you're ahead, you may want to reward yourself with a little spending spree, or change plans, dream bigger, or save more.

Review Your Goals—Your goals may change as the years pass. College tuition for the children may take precedence over a new car or a second home. Remember, this is only a financial blueprint—not a straitjacket. Don't be afraid to veer from the path as long as you stick to the main objectives of your long-term plan.

Getting from Point A to Point B

Once you have your goals on paper and you have a sense of where your money is going, you're ready to bring your financial blueprint to life. You can set up a monthly budget or a quarterly budget, whatever works better for you. The following worksheet will help you with your budgeting. Use it to keep track of your budgeted income and expenses versus the actual amount of money you spend and save. The more conscious you are of your budget and the ways you might stray from it, the more likely it is that you'll stick to it.

BUDGETING WORKSHEET

	Budget	Actual	(+/−) Budget vs. Actual
INCOME*			
Salary and wages	$	$	$
Self-employment income			
Retirement income			
Other income			
Total Income	$	$	$
EXPENSES			
Automobile	$	$	$
Charitable contributions			
Child care			
Clothing			
Dues/subscriptions			
Education			
Entertainment			
Food			
Gifts			
Home maintenance			
Insurance			
Investments			
Loans			
Medical/dental			
Mortgage/rent			
Retirement			
Savings			
Taxes			
Transportation			
Utilities			
Vacation			
Other			
Total Expenses	$	$	$
Total Income – Total Expenses = **BALANCE**	$	$	$

*Your budgeted income may differ from your actual income. For example, you may have switched jobs, lost your job, received a raise or didn't get an anticipated raise.

Selecting a Financial Advisor

Start Now!

Create your
Budgeting
Worksheet.

Log on to
hrblock.com/advisor

No one said you have to face the financial world alone. If you're following the advice in this book, you're putting together a very valuable blueprint for your financial future. But for some, a financial advisor can make the whole planning process much easier. Not every financial advisor is right for you. Selecting a financial advisor should be a personal, subjective process. An advisor who is perfect for one of your friends may be completely wrong for you. A good advisor takes each client's goals, risk tolerance, and personal needs into consideration.

If you're going to enlist the services of a professional in developing your financial plan, try to find one who is ideally suited to your needs. This financial advisor becomes a vital person in your life, helping you create the financial plan that will guide you toward the achievement of your financial goals. That's why you need a capable advisor who will help you make the best decisions. Over time, you may need to gather a team of other professional advisors, including an insurance professional, a financial advisor, an attorney, and a tax professional to assist you in managing your personal finances.

Find two or three prospective financial advisors by getting referrals from friends, doing some research, or by attending investment seminars sponsored by financial advisors. When you attend a seminar, if you like the advisor and agree with his or her basic philosophy, set up an appointment at his or her office. If you don't know anyone who has consulted an advisor, check with associations such as the Certified Financial Planner Board of Standards and the Financial Planning Association.

Meet with each prospective advisor and ask each one a series of questions to determine which one is the best fit for you. Here are some questions you can ask to help you find an advisor who will meet your needs:

**smart
step**

Respect the
time horizon
upon which
your financial
plan is based.
Resist the urge
to make hasty
or short-term
changes to a
long-term plan.

Types of Investors—"What types of individuals do you work with the most?" You want an advisor who is experienced at working with other individuals similar to yourself.

Approach—"What is your overall investment approach?" If the advisor has a well-conceived approach to financial planning and investing that appeals to you and seems to meet your needs, that's a definite plus. Ask for examples of financial plans and ask the advisor about periodic reviews of a person's financial plan. You want an advisor who will do more than produce a beautifully bound financial plan for you to keep on your coffee table. You want someone who will help you monitor all aspects of the plan, including your investment portfolio, insurance coverage, etc.

Services—"What types of services do you offer?" If the advisor specializes in options, futures, and speculative stocks, and you're looking for an advisor who can help you with a broad financial plan that would include investment products, tax planning, and insurance planning, that advisor would probably not be right for you. Find an advisor who specializes in the types of financial services and products that are of interest to you.

Experience—"How long have you been a financial advisor?" You probably don't need the most experienced advisor in the firm, as most of them may already have many clients and may not have enough time to spend with you. Ask the advisor to briefly describe his or her past work experience. Look for success under a variety of risk conditions.

Qualifications—"What qualifies you to give me financial advice and to develop my financial plan?" Ask about designations such as Certified Financial Planner™ (CFP) or Chartered Financial Consultant (ChFC). If you're purposely interviewing a specialized advisor, such as an insurance professional, estate planner, investment advisor, or stock broker, ask about insurance licenses and designations such as: Chartered Life Underwriter (CLU) or Accredited Estate Planner (AEP). Find out what trade organizations the financial advisor belongs to and ask about what he or she does to keep his or her education current. If the advisor is also a stock broker, he or she must also pass securities examinations administered by the **National Association of Securities Dealers** ◄........... (NASD).

Pay—"How are you compensated for your services?" Some financial advisors will help you put together a financial plan for a flat fee and leave it in your hands to do the rest. Others will help you work out a financial plan for free with the expectation of selling you the financial products to fulfill that plan, earning a commission on the sale of those products. You'll pay for the service either way, but you need to determine for yourself which type of advisor would better suit your needs.

The National Association of Securities Dealers (NASD) is a private, not-for-profit organization that governs the behavior of securities firms and representatives doing business with the public in the United States.

ADVISOR COMPENSATION AT A GLANCE

COMMISSION BASED

The advisor is paid based on transactions. The commission can be deducted from your total investment. Commissions are usually a percentage of the amount you invest in a product.

FEE BASED (FEE ONLY)

You pay a fee for service, usually based on the amount of time spent by the advisor, or by asset size. Some advisors charge a flat rate.

COMBINATION COMMISSION/FEE

Some advisors will use whichever method you prefer. If you choose an investment that pays them a commission, that amount is deducted from your total fee.

ASSET MANAGEMENT BASED

If you want an advisor to manage your money on an ongoing basis and do your investing for you, some will charge you a percentage of the amount of money they're managing. However, the amount of money required before he or she takes you on as a client can be significant.

THE CHALLENGE

Erika and Ivan, both in their late thirties, got married last year. Erika is a pharmacist and Ivan is a self-employed engineer. When they were single, each enjoyed spending their hard-earned money. They paid their bills on time, but never had anything left over for savings. One evening, Erika and Ivan talked about where they'd like to retire, probably someplace where it didn't snow. As they talked, they realized they were getting a very late start in planning for the future. In fact, Ivan said it was so unlikely that they'd be able to save enough that they might as well spend it as they go. Erika didn't agree, but the time wasn't right to discuss it. She wanted to look at their finances, but she didn't know where to start.

THE PLAN

The first thing Erika and Ivan had to do was to agree that they needed to do some planning. Erika decided to invite Ivan to join her at the senior center where she volunteered on Thursday nights. While there, Ivan talked to an eighty-year-old woman who described how she wasn't able to retire until ten years earlier because she hadn't planned very well for her retirement. Afterward, Ivan was more open to talking about planning because he didn't want to have to work until he was seventy. Erika went online and found some articles on personal finance. She also started a spending diary to track their money. It was hard because sometimes Ivan would get cash from the ATM and not recall exactly how he spent it. After several months, however, Ivan got on board and went through their checkbooks and the drawer where they kept their paid bills. He purchased personal finance software and started entering the data.

Pretty soon, they began to get a picture of their spending habits. They were earning plenty of money to fund their retirement dreams, but they just didn't have a plan in place to make their dreams a reality. As a first step, they decided to take advantage of the employer-match 401(k) plan at Erika's pharmacy and start saving toward the purchase of a retirement home on a monthly basis. While these were steps in the right direction for people who had never planned before, they also realized that they needed to do more.

"For our next step, we are going to find a qualified financial advisor," added Erika. "We both realized that we can make our dreams come true, but we're going to need some sound advice to make sure we stay on track."

Customer Service—Rather than asking what type of service the advisor will give you, set the agenda yourself, outlining the type of service you require. If you want the advisor to call you periodically, tell him or her and get him or her to agree to your terms in advance. Ask how the advisor will work with your other financial professionals, such as your tax professional or attorney. Find out if you'll be working exclusively with the person you're interviewing or if you'll be working with an assistant. If you aren't comfortable with the advisor's approach, say so.

If the advisor answers all of your questions to your satisfaction, that's a start. But also make sure that you have a good feeling about this person—that you have a good rapport, that you trust him or her, and that you feel you could enjoy a pleasant, long-term relationship with the advisor. Finally, you may want to do a little more checking.

For example, if the person you're interviewing is a stock broker, call the National Association of Securities Dealers (NASD) hotline (800-289-9999). There, you can find out if the advisor has ever been the subject of disciplinary action, a civil judgment, or a criminal conviction or indictment.

Working with an Advisor

Financial advisors can help you make realistic assumptions about your income needs, inflation rates, and investment returns. They can help you understand how one financial decision may affect others, and recommend specific investments based on your needs. They can also help keep you honest about making your plan and sticking to it .

Licensed financial professionals must abide by a code of conduct specific to their profession. For example, the Certified Financial Planner Board's *Code of Ethics and Professional Responsibility* describes the minimum standards of

smart step

If your advisor talks over your head about any products he or she is trying to sell you, or can't explain how those products work in terms you can understand, then you probably need to look for a different advisor.

smart step

Get a Social Security number for your baby right away. Any child you claim as a dependent on your income tax return must have a taxpayer identification number, regardless of age.

acceptable professional conduct for individuals authorized to use CFP certification marks, and CLUs must adhere to the *Code of Ethics of the American Society of Chartered Life Underwriters*.

The advisor's job is to simplify your life, not complicate it. You need an advisor you can trust, who is able to explain things to your satisfaction, and who puts your interests first.

When Life Changes

You may go through some dramatic changes in your life. A new baby, a divorce, a death in the family, or other significant developments could change life as you know it. When that happens, you'll need to update your vital information. Here are some key areas that will require your attention.

Legal concerns—Review your will, power of attorney, health-care proxies, and anything that names you as a beneficiary, such as a parent's will, family business documents, contracts, or deeds, to see whether you need to make provisions for your spouse or new baby.

Benefits—Update your retirement plan information, Social Security records, and, if necessary, Veterans Affairs to ensure that any benefits will go to the correct beneficiary. Make sure ownership and beneficiaries for checking and savings accounts, 401(k)s, and IRAs, are updated.

Tax status—Your tax withholding or estimated tax payments will need a second look, too. For instance, a new baby means you may be eligible for several additional tax breaks. Your tax professional can outline them for you.

Emergency contacts—Check your wallet to make sure the hospital emergency room knows who to call in case of an accident.

Insurance coverage—Review your insurance coverage to make sure it is appropriate for your personal situation. You don't want to find yourself uninsured or underinsured if you have a claim.

You should create a listing of personal information on yourself and all your family members (spouse, children, parents, siblings, etc.). If you keep it on your computer, keep a dated paper copy stored with the documents and records you gathered and organized earlier. Here's a checklist of what to include:

Contact Information—(for you and your relatives and your professional advisors, such as attorney, banker, executor, financial advisor, insurance professional, and tax professional) including:

- **Your name**
- **Address**
- **Phone**
- **Cell phone**
- **Fax**
- **E-mail address**
- **Social Security number**

Investment Records—Important information about various accounts and investments, including account numbers, contact information, and the name of the institution that holds your:

- **Annuities**
- **Bank accounts**

- **Bonds**
- **Business interests**
- **CDs**
- **Credit union acounts**
- **Child accounts**
- **Grandchild accounts**
- **Health insurance**
- **Life insurance**
- **Mutual funds**
- **Real estate**
- **Retirement accounts**
- **Safe deposit boxes**
- **Savings accounts**
- **Stocks**
- **Tax records**
- **Wills and trusts**

Certain myths prevent people from entering into the financial planning process. Don't let that happen to you. Once you have your goals in place, and have a good idea of how you're spending your money, you can create a budget that will move you in the right direction. A good financial advisor can be a tremendous help in forming and implementing your financial plan. If you want a financial advisor, use the procedures and questions described in this chapter to find one who is right for you.

the ESSENTIALS

1 You can put together a financial plan all at once or one piece at a time.

2 Different money management styles can derail the best financial plan. Talk with your partner about the differences in your skills, abilities, and relationships to money, and look for ways to use the differences to your mutual advantage.

3 Remember that you can adjust your plan if you need to. Better to have a plan and adjust it occasionally than to float through life with no plan at all.

4 Put together a listing of personal information about your family and your professional contacts and keep it in a safe and secure location.

smart step

Work with your advisor to adjust and rebalance your investment portfolio as your financial goals and objectives change over time.

3 [**BANKING ON SUCCESS:**

Exploring Your Options]

"Business and life are like a bank account—you can't take
out more than you put in."

—William Feather

Flashback to the 1970s: You're one of the first customers to go through the brand new drive-through lanes at your bank. No longer do you have to park the car and trudge through snow to go inside to make a deposit. So what if the speaker quality is a bit scratchy—you can hear the teller just fine. No longer do you have to plan your day to get to the bank between 8:30 a.m. and 3:00 p.m. The drive-through is open until 6:00 p.m., and there's a rumor in town that it will also be open on Saturday morning. What will they think of next?

We know now that technology exploded with innovations throughout the rest of the twentieth century (and into this one). The traditional bricks-and-mortar bank is still around, of course. But you can now choose to use the bricks-and-clicks bank or a virtual bank that's available only online. In fact, with online banking, you can complete almost every banking transaction without leaving home or wherever you may happen to be.

Choosing a Bank

Every sound financial plan starts with money in the bank. That's why it's important to choose a financial institution that not only offers a fair return on your deposit, but also provides the services and banking features you need to make your experience as convenient and comprehensive as possible.

There are many options from which to choose in selecting a financial institution. Traditional banks and savings and loans are the most popular, but millions of Americans also use credit unions or their brokerage firm for savings and checking services. And a growing number of consumers are banking online. Millions of Americans now pay bills and transfer funds on the Internet. Are you one of them yet? If not, you may want to consider giving it a try.

Before You Pick a Bank

Before you even begin comparison shopping for a new bank, it will help if you figure out exactly how you'll use your account. That way you can pick an account that will give you the best service and return on investment with the lowest possible fees.

Here are a few questions to answer before you begin your search:

- **How much will I start with and how much will I be adding each month?**
- **How much will I usually keep in my account?**
- **How many checks will I write each month?**
- **Do I want interest on my checking, and if so, am I willing to pay extra fees or maintain a higher balance for an account that pays interest?**
- **How important is it that I have a branch bank near my home, near my workplace, or both?**
- **How often will I be using automated teller machines (ATMs)?**
- **Will I be banking by telephone or computer?**
- **How important is personal service?**

The ideal bank would offer the perfect combination of convenience, low fees, high interest rates, and a broad menu of services that are right for you. Here are some factors to consider when selecting a bank:

ATM access—Millions of consumers do their banking almost entirely by automated teller machine. ATMs are convenient because they allow you to make deposits, withdrawals, and transfers, and check your account balances. (Some new machines even allow you to buy stamps, concert tickets, and other items.) And the standard ATM card will work in machines throughout the United States and around the world, so no matter where you travel, you'll always have access to your bank account. One problem, however, is that banks have been steadily increasing ATM fees for customers of other banks. If you use your own bank's ATMs, you pay no fee, but if you use the ATM of another bank, you may face fees

fast fact

Some banks reward customers who bank by ATM, phone, or computer by offering them lower-fee checking accounts.

If you have a
tendency to
overspend,
get overdraft
protection for
your checking
account. It will
save you money
and embarrass-
ment over
bounced checks.

of $2 or more on every transaction. So if you use ATMs often and in a variety of locations, it might pay to go with a larger bank that has more of its own ATMs available in your area. Many of the leading banks have ATMs in grocery stores, shopping centers, airports, health clubs, medical centers, and other convenient locations. The availability of ATMs shouldn't be the deciding factor in selecting a bank, but it is definitely something to consider when narrowing your choices.

Bank fees—Some banks have no account maintenance fees, no check-writing fees, free deposits, and no minimum balance requirement. Others charge fees for every check you write, every deposit you make, and every time your account falls below a certain level. The fees can eat away at your savings and checking accounts. Try to find the bank with the fewest and lowest fees for the services you'll need.

Location—With so many banks to choose from, you might as well stay close to home. Which banks have branches near your home (or, better yet, branches close to your home and workplace)? If you need to get to the bank on a regular basis, convenience is important. You don't want to drive across town every time you need to make a deposit. On the other hand, if you bank primarily through ATMs, twenty-four-hour telephone access, or the Internet, the bank's physical location is less important.

Interest rates—If you plan to open a savings account or interest-bearing checking account, find out which banks offer the highest interest rates. Bank savings account interest rates rarely come close to the rates you can get with corporate and government bonds, but there are definitely differences among banks. On a $100,000 savings account, a 1 percent difference in the interest rate can mean a $1,000 difference in your annual return. On the other hand, if you only plan to keep $5,000 or $6,000 in the bank, the interest rate difference may not be high enough to offset the difference in bank fees. A 1 percent difference in interest rates on a $5,000 account would only amount to about $50 a year. Make sure bank fees don't cost more than the difference.

Online options—Many banks have expanded their services to include online banking. You can check on your account balance, transfer funds, and pay bills online. Do you also need the option to download transaction information directly into personal finance software? More information on online banking is presented later in this chapter.

Other services—Banks are more than just a place to put your money. You can get a car loan, home loan, or other consumer or business loan through your bank, open a line of credit, make wire transfers, and, in some cases, buy stocks, bonds, or insurance polices, and get financial planning advice. Some banks even have investment specialists who can manage your money for you.

FDIC insured—All reputable banks (including virtual banks) are insured by the Federal Deposit Insurance Corporation (FDIC), which means that if anything should happen to the bank, your money is protected up to a maximum of $100,000. In truth, it would be extremely rare to lose money in a bank collapse, but it has happened. If you want to sleep a little better at night—and avoid a worst-case scenario—consider spreading your money around. But that's only if you have more than $100,000 in your accounts. Otherwise, keeping your money in one bank (FDIC insured) is probably the logical option.

Take it to the Bank

Once you've come up with your own profile of the services you'll need, and the amount of money you're ready to deposit, it's time to visit some banks—either in person or online. Most major banks have Web sites that will answer almost all of your questions about types of accounts available, minimum balances, and current interest rates. That could save you some driving time.

smart step

Check to see if your account's minimum balance is determined by the average balance over the month. If not, a one-day drop below the minimum will mean a penalty.

On the other hand, if you're the type of consumer who prefers to investigate things firsthand, you may want to visit several area banks and talk to bank representatives. Explain to the banker how you will be using the account and how much you plan to deposit, and the banker should be able to suggest an ideal account for you.

Here is a list of questions to ask a prospective banker:

- **What types of accounts are available?**
- **What are the yields on the savings, interest-bearing checking, and money market accounts?** Banks are required to give you the **annual percentage yield** (APY) so you can compare apples with apples.
- **On accounts that pay interest, how often is the interest compounded?** The more often the better, preferably daily.
- **What fees, charges, or penalties will I be subject to, and when do they apply?**
- **How many ATMs does the bank have locally that I can use for free?**
- **Is the bank tied in with a national network of ATMs that will give me a break on the fees when I'm not using my own bank's ATM?**
- **Does the bank have online banking and bill paying?** What fees apply to those services?
- **If I need to call a banker to check on my account, is there a number I can use to reach a live person?** Some banks don't always list the phone numbers for their branch offices. When you select a bank and open an account, ask your banker for a phone number. Then write it down where you can find it later. Someday, for some reason, you *will* want that number.

A bank account is an essential tool in a sound financial plan, so choose carefully. Selecting a convenient bank with the right services, a minimum of fees, and a competitive interest rate is one of your first steps on the path to a solid financial future.

plain talk

The annual percentage yield (APY) is the total return on your money. It includes compounded interest and is the best way to compare yields on savings accounts.

Credit Unions—You could also consider banking at a credit union. If you're a member of an organization that has a credit union or work at a business with a credit union, that might be your best banking option. Credit unions offer many of the same features and services as banks, usually with lower fees. They also often offer higher interest rates on your savings and lower interest rates on your consumer loans. And many credit unions offer mutual funds and retirement plans.

Credit unions don't need the extra profit margins that banks require because they are essentially owned and operated by their customers, and they're in business for the explicit purpose of serving those customers. Share-draft accounts offered by credit unions function like basic checking accounts, but are open only to members of the organization that runs the credit union. Credit unions also are federally insured so your money is as safe there as money in an FDIC-insured bank.

The Right Checking Account

smart step

Check whether the interest is paid on your balance every day (the ideal), the average monthly balance, or the lowest balance each month. The differences can add up.

Banks, savings and loans, and other financial services companies keep developing more and more ways to attract your business. The options can seem overwhelming. But if you do your research, you can find a checking account with the right level of services at a minimal cost.

Here is a list of some of the types of checking accounts available for you to consider:

- **Basic checking.** With this type of account, you don't get interest on your money, but you can usually write as many checks as you want. You'll probably have to pay a monthly fee unless you maintain a minimum balance.
- **Free checking with interest.** Many banks offer free checking with interest if you're willing to maintain a fairly high minimum balance. The balance

If you need to withdraw money from a CD before it reaches maturity, you'll probably pay a penalty. The penalty is tax deductible.

requirement varies by the bank, but it is typically in the range of $1,500 to $2,500.

- **High-balance account.** You may be able to get a higher interest rate and more free services if you can keep more money in your account. Some banks offer free checking, free online bill paying, free ATM usage, and a higher interest rate if you're willing to keep more than $5,000 in the account at all times, or if you're willing to keep at least $50,000 combined in your savings and checking accounts.

- **Linked account.** A linked account includes both a checking account and a savings account. The bank may lower or eliminate its monthly fees if you maintain a minimum balance in one, the other, or both. It may also be offered as a package with other bank services, such as a credit card.

- **No-frills or lifeline accounts.** These accounts often have a low minimum initial deposit, low minimum balances, and low or no monthly fees. However, a no-frills account will probably limit the number of checks you can write or deposits you can make without paying additional fees. Some no-frills accounts are geared to online banking. If all deposits are done by direct deposit—for example, by your employer—the account may allow unlimited checks, a low minimum balance, and low or no monthly fees, but charge extra if you use a teller.

- **Senior citizen or student accounts.** Banks often offer special accounts for senior citizens or students, which provide perks such as free checks or discounts on consumer items. Some banks do not pay interest on such accounts, but others offer an interest-bearing negotiable order of withdrawal (NOW) account that does pay interest. The rate can be fixed or variable, and it usually increases for higher balances.

- **Asset management account.** An asset management account is an investment account that lets you write checks drawn on it. Your money is typically kept in an interest-bearing money market account and you can write checks to access your funds. Income from any investments automatically goes into that account. The minimum balance and annual fee can be steeper than for other types of checking accounts.

More for Your Savings

For the money you won't need to spend right away, a savings account is one option worth exploring. There are many other savings options, but even your local bank should have a few choices for your long-term savings. Here are some of the more popular savings plan options:

Passbook Accounts—Passbook accounts have low initial deposit and low minimum balance requirements. This is an option if your savings are pretty slim. However, interest rates are comparatively low.

Statement Savings Accounts—Statement savings accounts are more convenient than passbook accounts, but generally pay a low interest rate. Often linked to checking accounts, they can help meet minimum balances. You can also use a statement savings account to park your dollars until you can build up a higher balance that can earn you better interest elsewhere. Like passbook accounts, statement savings accounts are protected by FDIC insurance.

Certificates of Deposit (CDs)—In addition to savings accounts, financial institutions also offer certificates of deposit with varying lengths of maturity. If you can tie up your money for several months or several years, you may be able to get a higher rate of return from CDs than you would get with typical savings accounts. This is not always the case, particularly with short-term CDs. Not only do they tend to pay lower interest than the longer-term CDs, they sometimes pay a lower rate than you would get with a money market account. It pays to compare your options and to shop around. Some financial institutions offer higher CD rates than others.

One drawback: CDs are not liquid as are savings and checking accounts. You can only get your money out when the CD matures (unless you're willing to pay

smart step

Don't open a savings account that requires a minimum balance if you think you may have trouble maintaining it. Penalties and charges can wipe out any extra interest it earns and can even cost you money in the end.

a penalty—which minimizes or eliminates any interest you would get from the CD). Typically, CDs are offered in amounts of $1,000, $5,000, $10,000, and up. Like savings accounts, bank CDs are generally FDIC-insured.

Money Market Accounts—Money market accounts offer an interest rate that fluctuates regularly along with the market for short-term securities. But the money market accounts generally pay higher interest than standard savings accounts. They also usually require a higher minimum deposit and balance. You are sometimes allowed to write checks on the account, with some restrictions. Generally, a money market account is a good place to park your money while awaiting a move to a more long-term investment.

Online Banking

Bricks-and-mortar banks that also have Web sites are sometimes called clicks-and-mortar banks. If you are online already, already use (or are thinking of using) a personal finance software program, and have numerous bills to pay each month, definitely consider completing more transactions via online banking. Today, few banks charge for individual account access online, and if they charge for online bill payment, the monthly fee is around $5.

Here are some advantages of banking online:

- **It's convenient.** The bank is open twenty-four hours a day.
- **You have access to detailed information about your accounts.** For example, you can determine what checks are still outstanding.
- **You can double-check ATM cash withdrawals, as well as debit card purchases and other unentered transactions.** If you're like most people, you sometimes overlook checkbook entries. It's helpful to be able to check them online.

- **You can bank from anywhere as long as you have access to the Internet.**
- **You can transfer funds from one online account to another, or make a payment on any loan or credit card account at your bank.** For example, if it's two days before your credit card payment is due, you can transfer funds from your checking account and avoid steep late payment fees.
- **You can download transaction information into your personal finance software.**
- **You can pay bills online.**
- **You can apply for loans online.**

Banks that have no physical branches are also an option for you to consider—In a sense, these "virtual" banks exist entirely on the Internet. Because they save money by not having buildings or tellers, they can pay higher yields, charge lower fees, and require lower minimum amounts for accounts. One drawback is that virtual banks have no ATMs. You also have to deposit checks by mail or transfer money from another account, unless the virtual bank has made arrangements with regional ATM networks to allow account holders to make deposits at machines. And if you have a problem, you'll have to resolve it online or by telephone.

The Future is Now

B anking technology is changing, even as you read this book. Electronic Check Conversion (ECC), voice authentication, a mouse that reads your thumbprint, ATMs that use facial, iris, or fingerprint scans—all of these innovations are in your future. In fact, you may have already encountered them in pilot programs.

smart step

If you're shopping for a new bank, look around to see which local bank has the most ATMs located where you need them the most.

THE CHALLENGE

At thirty-five, Phil has a busy lifestyle. A computer programmer, he works at least 60 hours a week. Three nights a week, he exercises at the gym for an hour to reduce stress. On Friday nights he goes dancing, and the rest of the weekend he spends time with friends or playing golf. He finds himself putting bank statements on his desk and never looking at them. And sometimes he forgets to pay bills and ends up with hefty late payment penalties. Phil wants to simplify how he does his banking and is considering a move from traditional banking to online banking.

THE PLAN

The first thing Phil needs to do is determine whether online banking is right for him. He is already comfortable with computers, so that's no problem. Because he writes a lot of checks each month (fifteen to twenty), he will benefit from paying bills online. To find out about specific online services and fees that his bank offers, Phil can either drop by the bank to talk with an online banking specialist or visit his bank's Web site. After he is sure he wants to switch to online banking, he may consider purchasing personal money management software. He'll be able to access his accounts without the software, but if he wants to download financial information to his computer, he'll want the software. Tutorials in the software will help him learn how to download financial information directly into the software. And his bank's Web site may have a Frequently Asked Questions (FAQs) section to guide him through the process.

For obvious reasons, banks and merchants want to minimize losses from bad checks and insufficient funds. With ECC, you write a check and it's processed like a debit or credit card. When you make a payment with a check, it's run through a check reader that gathers the check number, your account number, and your financial institution's identification number. The cashier enters the check amount on a terminal keypad and the check is approved. The clerk hands the voided check back to you with a receipt. Depending on the system, there may be an immediate debit to your account, or the funds may be debited within two days.

Passwords and personal identification numbers (PINs) could be replaced by voice authentication systems. The bank will match your voice to the one on file for you. If there is a match, you have access. No more worries about stolen passwords and PINs. Because your voice is as unique as your fingerprint, your accounts will be more secure. A device called a thumbprint mouse could eliminate the need for PINs in online banking. The mouse scans your thumb print and matches specific characteristics against a template set up for you. And like security systems already installed in buildings, facial, iris, or fingerprint scans will be the way you gain access to ATMs.

A bank that serves your financial needs in a convenient and secure way is one solid stone in your financial plan's foundation. Use the information in this chapter to help you find a bank that offers all of the services you need or may want access to in the future.

fast fact

Unlike a money market mutual fund, a money market account at a bank or savings and loan is insured by the FDIC.

smart step

Start Now!

Chart how fast
your savings
can grow.

Log on to
hrblock.com/advisor

the ESSENTIALS

1 When selecting a checking account, shop around for an account that meets your needs with a minimum of fees and, when possible, a competitive interest rate. Look for a convenient location—driving miles for a small increase in interest may not be worth the expense to get there.

2 Know what you need from your account, and compare accounts based on how much money you expect to keep in it, how frequently you'll write checks and make deposits, and whether any extra services or higher interest rates are worth the extra fees.

3 Savings accounts offer security. Compare their returns based on the annual percentage yield, which includes the effect of compounding interest.

4 Banking online can be safe, convenient, and inexpensive. You may be able to access all your accounts (checking, savings, CDs, mortgage loans, and lines of credit) to manage them instead of going to a bank.

problem or in error. You can order a copy of your credit report and credit score from any of the three major credit reporting bureaus:

- **Experian** (888-EXPERIAN or www.experian.com)
- **TransUnion** (800-888-4213 or www.transunion.com)
- **Equifax** (800-685-1111 or www.equifax.com)

An explanation of how to read the report is included. You can also order a 3-in-1 report that merges reports from the three bureaus.

What if You're Turned Down?

If you're turned down for a loan or credit card, ask why before you give up.

- **If it's a problem with your credit history, you may be able to fix it by contacting the credit bureau that issued the report or the merchant that reported the problem.** You're entitled to include an explanation of up to one hundred words in your credit file for any entry that's a problem. If you were late paying a bill because you were in the hospital when it arrived, tell the credit bureau. It may take time and effort to clean up your credit report, but it's worth it. After all, this is your financial alter ego—and it's the person creditors see when considering your application.
- **If at first you don't succeed, try, try again.** Different lenders have different standards. In fact, there are specialty lenders and credit card companies that cater specifically to customers with poor credit histories. But there is a price to pay. Those companies are in the high-risk end of the business, and they charge higher interest rates and stiffer late fees. If you're a credit risk, you may be able to get a credit card from a company like that—with the higher interest charges, lower credit limit, and other restrictions that go along with it.
- **Clear up your other credit problems, pay your credit card bills on time, and keep your other bills current.** Maybe the next time you apply for credit, the terms you receive will be better.

fast fact

If you're turned down for credit, you're entitled to a free copy of your credit report. Residents of some states are entitled to a free copy once a year.

smart step

Manage your credit cards wisely by paying the balance in full and on time every month.

If You Have Good Credit

Here are some terms to look for in a credit card:

No annual fees—Why get a card that charges an annual fee when it's just as easy to get one that doesn't? Sometimes, to get a card that offers bonus miles or merchandise points, you have to pay an annual fee. But make sure you're getting your money's worth. If you charge only $4,000 a year on a card with a $50 annual fee, and it takes 25,000 points for a free flight, you might as well get a different card, save the annual fee, and pay for the flight yourself. But if you charge $10,000 to $20,000 (or more) a year, a bonus card could be well worth the fee.

Lowest interest rate—Rates vary from month to month and year to year. To find the best rate, you need to do some comparison shopping. Look for an interest rate that is no higher than the prime rate plus 5 percent—and you may be able to do even better than that. But if you pay the balance in full every month, this isn't a factor.

Extra benefits—As long as you're using a credit card, you might as well get something extra from it. Many cards offer you cash back, frequent flier miles, or bonus points for free merchandise.

Low late fees—If you get stuck with a late fee, the lower the better. Some card companies charge $35 or more per month if you miss a payment—even on a bill of just a few dollars. Find a card with late fees of $15 or less.

Late fee exemptions—If you generally pay your credit card bill on time, some companies will waive the late fee on the rare occasions that you do miss a payment. That is a feature worth shopping for. (You'll still have to pay any additional finance charges, of course.)

Your good credit is worth a lot—but only if you shop around to make it pay off for you.

Handling Debt

D ebt is not all bad. In fact, assuming debt is the only way to build a track record of dealing with debt. The debt itself is not the problem. The problem is its overuse, misuse, and abuse.

There's a simple rule for dealing wisely with debt, especially credit card debt: Pay your bills on time. Pay the whole thing. Every month. And if you can't afford to pay it off every month, quit using your credit card. Using a credit card to buy merchandise that you couldn't afford to buy with cash is one of the most common ways to bury yourself in debt. You'll thank yourself later if you stop spending until your debts are paid.

Some consumers feel they've done well if they send in the minimum credit card payment each month. That's no way to deal with debt. In fact, it's a good way to stay buried in debt. Your balance will steadily rise, and so will your monthly interest payments. Cut your activities, cut your expenses, and catch up financially before your debt gets out of hand. Many casual credit card users run up balances of $50,000 to $100,000—or more. That's a financial burden from which they might never recover.

——————————————— **Getting the Monkey off Your Back**
Assume that you have a credit card balance of $2,000 with an annual percentage rate (APR) of 18 percent. The following illustration shows the difference between paying only the minimum required, paying extra, and paying the full amount.

smart step

Buy only what you can afford, and pay your bills in full, on time, every time.

	IF YOU PAY ONLY THE MINIMUM REQUIRED	IF YOU PAY EXTRA	IF YOU PAY IN FULL WHEN THE BILL ARRIVES
Minimum monthly payment	$ 50.00	$ 50.00	$ 50.00
Additional monthly payment	$ 0.00	$ 25.00	$1,950.00
Interest rate charged	18%	18%	18%
Time it will take to pay off $2,000	5 years, 2 months	2 years, 11 months	1 month
Total interest paid on $2,000	$1,077.24	$ 573.35	$ 0.00
Total cost of item	$3,077.24	$2,573.35	$2,000.00

If more than 36 percent of your take-home pay is earmarked for debt, including your home mortgage, then you're probably spending above your means. Cut back on your expenses and reduce your debt.

Even if you only make the minimum payment, at least pay it on time. One or more late fees could wind up costing you as much or more than the interest. Plus, a pattern of late payments can be a blemish on your records with lenders. If you really get into serious debt trouble, timely payments could be the lone bright spot on your record—and it does help.

When You're Buried in Debt

If you're already in debt over your head, here are some strategies for improving the situation:

- **Minimize your new debt by radically reducing your spending.** No frills, no travel, no electronic gadgets until your debt is under control. Think seriously about canceling and cutting up all your credit cards and paying cash for everything.
- **Pay more than the minimum.** If the minimum payments on your credit cards total $225 a month, could you pay $350 or $400 a month? If you're reducing spending, you should have additional funds to pay down your debt.
- **Consolidate your debt.** If you can consolidate all of your credit card bills onto one credit card with a low interest rate, do it. Paying off your 18 percent

credit card bills by transferring the balance to a credit card with 9 percent interest will cut your monthly interest payments in half.

- **Negotiate with creditors.** Creditors may be willing to extend your payments if you discuss why you're having problems and show them exactly how you plan to pay them back. But if you can get them to agree to revised payments, be prepared to stick to your part of the deal; they're less likely to be flexible the second time around.

- **Try dividing credit card debt into two types: little stuff and big stuff.** Use a no-fee card for convenience, put the little stuff on it, and pay the whole thing monthly. If you know you'll need several months to pay for something big—a new refrigerator, for instance—put it on a card that advertises low (or no) interest payments for the first six months you have it. Pay the loan off completely by the end of the low-interest period. Then, cancel the card.

- **Consider using your savings to get out of debt.** If you have money in the bank earning 5 percent while you're paying 18 percent on a credit card balance, use your savings to pay the bill. That saves you 13 percent interest every month. On a large debt over the course of a year, that can mean several hundred dollars in savings. For example, on a debt of $10,000, over the course of a year you would save $1,300. However, don't use all of your savings to pay off credit cards. Always have funds for an emergency available.

Debt Consolidation—Sometimes borrowing more money from one lender is cheaper than borrowing smaller amounts from a lot of lenders—especially if you can get a lower interest rate for the new loan. Sticking with one lender also reduces the number of late fees, annual fees, and other charges you might have with multiple lenders.

If you're thinking about consolidating debts, try to set up a schedule you can stick with that will pay the debt off as quickly as possible. That may be several months or several years, but the sooner you pay off your debts, the better off you'll be.

smart step

To avoid late-payment fees, either pay bills each week as they come in, or try to switch the date when your bill is issued so you can pay all bills once a month.

When shopping for loans, compare apples to apples. Use the **annual percentage rate** (APR), which is a truer measure of the cost of borrowing than the interest rate alone. Also, there's a broad variance in what lenders charge. It definitely pays to shop around.

Transferring Balances—Some consumers switch credit cards every time they get a mailing that offers to charge no interest on balances transferred from another card. If you're disciplined enough to stay ahead of the switching game, that can save you a lot of interest payments over the long term.

There are, however, a couple of pitfalls with that approach. If you don't switch cards at the right time, the interest rate will automatically shoot up to normal levels. And that goes on your credit report, which will be a red flag for future lenders. One alternative would be to tell your current credit card company that you're switching to a card with better terms. They may offer you a better rate to keep your business, but they probably won't match the interest-free rate you might get for a few months as part of a special promotion for a different card.

Starting Over

Whether you are completely out of debt, or have simply resolved to change your ways, there are certain steps you can take to increase your odds of staying financially afloat and maintaining a solid credit rating in the future.

If you know you have trouble with credit cards, but want to begin reestablishing a good credit record, get a secured card, which limits your spending to a percentage of the money you deposit to get the card. Consider keeping the card at home in a safe place instead of carrying it with you so spending won't

plain talk

The annual percentage rate (APR) includes not only the interest rate you're being charged, but also any fees and other charges imposed by the lender.

GETTING CREDIT			
	HOW IT WORKS	**ADVANTAGES**	**DISADVANTAGES**
Credit Card	▪ Allows you to make purchases without using cash ▪ May or may not require that entire balance be paid monthly	▪ Convenient ▪ Allows greatest flexibility in spending ▪ Can help establish good credit record ▪ Limited liability for fraud and misuse by others	▪ Makes overspending easier ▪ Revolving credit interest can add up rapidly ▪ Paying only minimum balance can mean long-term debt ▪ Interest and fees
Debit Card	▪ Automatically subtracts spending from your bank account	▪ Convenient ▪ Can help limit spending to the money in your account ▪ In some cases, may also be used as a credit card	▪ Greater need to balance checkbook to avoid bouncing checks ▪ If lost, gives thief easier access to your bank account
Secured Card	▪ Requires money deposited in advance in a bank account; your credit limit is based on your deposit	▪ Convenient ▪ Can help control overspending ▪ Can help reestablish good credit	▪ Requires cash up front ▪ Interest rates can be high ▪ Not paying the bill can mean losing your initial deposit

smart step

If you're up-to-date on all loans, you can consolidate them—once. But check to see if a longer term, even at a lower rate, means more total interest, and if it does, decide whether that's right for you.

be a spontaneous decision. Or get a debit card, which automatically deducts your expenses from your checking account every time you use the card.

If you use a debit card, write every charge in your checkbook to help you track what you're spending. Don't spend what you don't have, and pay bills on time—in full, every month.

As you pay down your debt, keep a running tally of your progress. Then start building your emergency fund so revolving credit won't be your only fallback position.

Home Equity

There are a couple of major reasons to consider borrowing against the equity in your home if you're struggling with consumer debt. First, the interest rate is usually lower. Of course, the reason it's lower is because the lender has something to go after if you default: your home. Also, the interest is tax deductible, usually on indebtedness of up to $100,000 or on the **equity** you have in your home, whichever is less. Interest on consumer debt such as credit card bills and car loans isn't.

Aside from selling your home outright, there are three good ways to squeeze cash from your home equity:

1. **Refinance.** If interest rates have dropped since you bought the home, you may be able to get a new mortgage with a lower interest rate. That can save you thousands of dollars over the course of the mortgage. It can also give you a chance to get a check from the bank for part of your equity, and have the amount of that payment rolled into the new mortgage. You can then pay off your other debts, leaving you with only a monthly mortgage to pay. And if the new interest rate is significantly lower than the old rate, you could end up with a lower payment or a shorter time frame—even after tacking your other debt onto the original mortgage debt. On the other hand, if interest rates have stayed about the same or gone up, refinancing probably isn't the right option. Generally, interest rates should be 1 to 2 percentage points less than your current rate to make refinancing worthwhile. For a more accurate estimate, use one of the many online calculators that can help you analyze your situation.

2. **Second mortgage.** You can get a loan in the form of a second mortgage or home equity loan. As with the first mortgage, you are borrowing a fixed amount and paying it back over a specific period of time. But because second mortgages tend to be riskier than the original mortgage, you will pay a slightly higher interest rate—but still much lower than a typical credit card or consumer loan rate. Furthermore, you'll be making a second monthly payment.

plain talk

When you own something, you have equity in it. Home equity is the difference between what you owe on your mortgage and what the home is worth on the market.

3. **Home equity line of credit.** You could also use the equity in your home to set up a line of credit. This works a little differently. When you open a line of credit for a certain amount, you can draw from it when and as you need it for any amount up to the specified limit. You generally pay interest only on the amount you borrow, and you pay it back according to the terms of the line of credit, but you are not required to pay on the principal each month—only the interest. There are a couple of dangers associated with a home equity line of credit— especially if you have a history of handling credit poorly. With a line of credit, there's no set pay-off date. The loan can linger with you indefinitely unless you resolve to pay it off. Plus, with that open line of credit sitting there untouched, there is always the temptation to tap into it just like credit card debt. This time, however, it's your home that's on the line, so you can't afford to lose control of this debt.

smart step

Start Now!

Compare your options for using the equity in your home.

Log on to hrblock.com/advisor

When you're comparing a loan to a line of credit, be sure to add up all the costs. The APR for a loan usually includes costs and charges associated with the loan; the APR for a line of credit may not. Unless you include them for both, it's not a fair comparison.

Eliminating Student Debt

If you're a recent college graduate, you may owe thousands of dollars on your student loans. Chances are, you will struggle for a while, but paying your student loans on time should be a top priority. By doing so, you can quickly establish a strong credit rating.

You don't want to default on your student loan for several reasons. In addition to damaging your credit record, you also might have your paycheck garnisheed to cover the loan. And if you default on a student loan, you will owe the full amount immediately. A default on a student loan would also mean you couldn't

THE CHALLENGE

George and Alice love the old home they purchased ten years ago. It took a lot of work, but they finally have it renovated. They purchased the home for $80,000 and still owe about $70,000 on their original 30-year mortgage. However, thanks to their renovations and a rising housing market, their home is now worth $110,000 on the open market.

"You would think the increase in our home's value would make us a financially happy couple, but that wasn't the case at all," said George. "We charged a lot of building materials on our credit cards, and found ourselves paying only the minimum payment each month." "Plus," added Alice, "we took a couple of nice vacations and used our credit cards to pay for them, too."

Even though both George and Alice have good jobs, they were struggling to meet their financial obligations, and the stress that put on their marriage was taking a toll. "We were arguing more than we like to admit, and almost every argument was about money," said Alice.

THE PLAN

George and Alice realized they had about $40,000 equity in their home. They consulted a mortgage lender to see if they could use some of the equity to ease their financial situation. They discovered that by refinancing their home and incorporating all their credit card debt into the new loan, they could reduce their total monthly payments considerably. The new home loan was at a rate of 6 percent, compared to the 18 percent interest they were paying on their credit card balances. And, they were pleased to learn, the interest was tax deductible.

"We were thrilled," said Alice. "But, at the same time, we realized that we needed to adjust our spending habits. If we went back to running up our credit card balances, we'd be in worse trouble than ever, and could even risk losing our home."

The couple took a drastic but worthwhile step. They cut up all their credit cards but one, and put that one in their safe deposit box for emergencies. For everything else, including vacations, they would pay cash. "The new spending life style took a bit of getting used to, but now we love the idea of having just one debt that we're working hard to pay off. Now, we can get back to fighting about relatives like everyone else," joked George.

qualify for a low-interest HUD (U.S. Housing and Urban Development) loan or VA (U.S. Veterans Administration) loan on a home. Also, the federal government can keep any income tax refund you had coming to partially satisfy the debt. So there are many reasons to keep paying on that student loan.

If the student loan is a serious drain on your finances, there may be a few things you can do to improve your situation:

Consolidation—With consolidation, loan agencies agree to accept smaller monthly payments, typically by extending the life of the loan past the usual ten years. You'll pay more interest in the long run, but it's better than defaulting. If you have a federal loan, you can consolidate using the government's Direct Consolidation Loan program, which averages the interest rates on the existing loans to come up with the new rate. Otherwise, you may be able to work with a commercial lender. Consolidation also may make sense if interest rates are lower than they were when you took out the original loans.

Cancellation—You may qualify to have part of your loans canceled if you work in certain occupations. For example, up to $5,000 of a Stafford loan can be canceled if the student serves in the military or teaches in a low-income school for five years after graduation. Child-care providers and nurses also may be eligible. Loans can also be canceled if the school closes or falsely certifies the loan, or if the student becomes permanently and totally disabled or dies.

Forbearance—In some cases, you may be able to make reduced payments or defer making payments. If your lender grants a forbearance on your loan, your payments will be postponed or reduced, but the loan will still continue to accumulate interest during that time.

fast fact

You can generally deduct up to $2,500 of student loan interest you pay annually, and you don't even have to itemize deductions. Your tax professional can explain the details.

smart step

Check every June to see whether student loan interest rates, which change every July, will be lower for the next year. If so, consolidating your loans will lock in that lower rate.

What if You've Already Defaulted?

Even if you've already defaulted, it still may be possible to work your way back into good standing. Lending agencies can help work out a repayment schedule. You will need to supply documented evidence of your inability to pay, such as pay stubs and bills. Make monthly payments regularly for a year and the loan will be taken out of default, the blemish on your credit record will be deleted, and you'll qualify once again for additional student financial aid.

Bankruptcy

If all else fails, there's always bankruptcy. It's not pleasant and it will leave a blemish on your credit record for years, but bankruptcy may be the only answer if you've explored every other logical alternative. When you file for bankruptcy, your debts are frozen. What happens next depends on the type of bankruptcy you file under: Chapter 7 or Chapter 13 (so-called because those are the sections of the bankruptcy code applying to individuals that set up the procedures).

In a Chapter 13 bankruptcy, you lose no property, but you'll have to follow a court-approved plan for paying what you owe over several years. Chapter 13 basically shields you from your creditors while you get out from under the debt. Chapter 7 involves liquidating all assets that are not exempt. Exempt property may include cars, work-related tools, and basic household furnishings. Some property may be sold by a court-appointed official (a trustee) or turned over to creditors. Certain debts are wiped out completely, but the bankruptcy filing will remain on your credit report for up to ten years.

Bankruptcy doesn't excuse you from child support or alimony, taxes, some student loans, or any big purchases you made just before filing (so forget about a last-minute spending spree before you file—those debts will not be eliminated). However, in most states, you'll be able to retain your retirement accounts, pensions, at least some home equity, personal items such as clothing and furniture, and sometimes your car.

You Can Do It

Almost everyone incurs debt at certain points in life. Debt may be necessary to finance a college education, pay emergency expenses, or purchase a home or car. The wise use of debt can actually increase your financial security, as when you borrow to pay for a college education and watch the borrowed money return many fold in the form of higher lifelong earnings.

But debt can also be your financial enemy. If you borrow for the wrong reasons, such as to purchase entertainment equipment or to finance a vacation, you can quickly find yourself in financial difficulty. When you need to borrow, be a wise consumer and shop diligently for the lowest interest rate and ideal payment schedule for your needs. And, we'll say it once more, pay off those credit card bills in full every month.

smart step

If you've decided to file for bankruptcy, contact an attorney and a tax professional *before* you file.

fast fact

Rolling debt into your home puts your home at risk if you default on the loan. Be sure you'll be able to pay off the new loan before you put your home at risk.

1 Pay your credit card bills on time, every month, in full. Revolving credit card debt and late fees mount quickly, and your track record will affect your ability to get loans in the future.

2 Remember that all debt is not created equal. Some kinds of debt have both lower interest rates and tax advantages that can help reduce the amount you'll pay overall.

3 If you see you're heading for trouble, don't postpone tackling it. The sooner you begin working your way out of debt, the easier it will be. Ask for help *before* you need it.

4 A home equity loan might help you consolidate your debts and provide you with tax savings as well.

5 Filing Chapter 7 or Chapter 13 bankruptcy is an option if there is absolutely no way out of your debt load. Be aware of the consequences of doing so.

5 [SAVING GRACE:

Smart Steps to Bigger Savings]

"The secret of financial success is to spend what you have
  left after saving instead of saving what you have left after
  spending."

—Anonymous

If someone offered you $1,000 today or $1,000 in a year, what would you do? Take the money now, of course. You can put the $1,000 to work for you today and end up with more than $1,000 in a year. The sooner you begin putting money aside, the sooner you'll become financially secure, and the more savings you'll have over the long term. It's a concept known as the **time value of money**, and it is one of the most alluring aspects of finance.

Through the magic of compounding, an investment can grow exponentially over a period of years. For example, if you invested $1,000 in a CD at the beginning of 1994 and that investment grew 5 percent each year, the initial $1,000 investment would have grown to more than $1,600 by the end of 2003. But if you had waited until the beginning of 2001 to invest, your $1,000 investment would only have grown to only $1,158 by the end of 2003. That's the time value of money. It's a principle you can use to your advantage for your own savings plan.

Time vs. Inflation

Time and money face two opposing forces. While one force, the time value of money, keeps your investments growing and compounding year after year, the other force, inflation, steadily dilutes the value of every dollar you own.

With its seemingly endless cycle of increasing prices for goods and services, inflation erodes the buying power of your money. And the higher the inflation rate, the faster the value of the dollar declines. That's why investors strive to receive a return on their investments that is higher than the rate of inflation. It's the only way to achieve greater wealth with your existing dollars. In fact, if your money isn't growing, you're actually losing ground to inflation.

For those who are already set for life, a return that keeps pace with **inflation** is probably adequate. But for those of us who are saving for retirement, a new home, or a college education for the children, matching the rate of inflation just isn't good enough. If you don't get a return rate on your savings somewhat above the rate of inflation, your quest for financial security will be like jogging endlessly on a treadmill.

To find your real rate of return on savings or investments, subtract the inflation rate from the rate of return you're getting. For example, if the inflation rate is 4 percent and the rate of return on an investment is 8.5 percent, your real rate of return is only 4.5 percent.

A Saving Mentality

S tarting a savings plan isn't easy—especially considering the alternative. Spending money on new clothes, home furnishings, and electronics, a better car, concerts, ball games, or trips to far-off destinations is so much more fun and exciting than depositing a check in the bank or transferring money from your checking account to a savings account. But you can have it both ways—money in the bank and the ability to buy the things you want—in moderation. First, however, you need to pay yourself. Give yourself the peace of mind and the control of your financial life that only a solid savings plan can offer.

The savings discipline is really just a mindset. It's you, taking control of your spending impulses, recognizing the long-term picture, and making a subtle change in your money mentality. What is that change? Instead of spending first and saving second, pay yourself first, with a deposit into your savings account, and use the dollars you have left to buy the things you want.

plain talk

Inflation is a broad-based increase in the cost of goods and services. An inflation rate of 3 percent, for example, means the average price of goods and services is climbing by 3 percent a year.

When thinking
about saving,
always think in
terms of paying
current taxes or
deferring taxes
as well as saving
for short-term,
intermediate, or
long-term goals.

It's your decision: Consume now or consume later. In Chapter 2, you took the time to quantify (put in dollars and time) your financial goals. Now it's time to act, so you can take advantage of compounding. Whether it's saving for your child's college education, a trip to Hawaii, a summer home near the lake, or an early retirement, you have to put your mind to it and develop a saving mentality. It can be a challenge just to cover everyday expenses, let alone put money away for something in the future. Yet, the earlier you start saving for your intermediate and long-term goals, the easier it is to accumulate the money you'll need.

We can't emphasize this point enough. The longer you wait to start saving, the more of your own hard-earned dollars you'll have to use to build your child's college fund, your vacation fund, or your retirement fund. Use the power of time and compounding! Start early and generate the funds for the majority of your goals through your return on investment—the interest rate or capital appreciation you receive on the money you invest. In fact, if you start early enough, you could theoretically stop saving entirely at some point and still be far ahead of most people who delay their savings plan until later in life.

The Power of Compounding

For example, let's say you put $1,000 in a savings account on your twentieth birthday, and did the same thing on your birthday every year for the next ten years. After that, you stopped adding anything to the account, but left what was there alone. Your friend, however, waited until he was thirty to start putting $1,000 a year away, and didn't stop until he was sixty-five. Both of you earned the same rate of return the whole time.

Amazing as it may seem, even though you only saved for ten years while your friend saved for thirty-five years, you would still have more money at age sixty-five than your friend.

COASTING ON AN EARLY START		
YEAR	STARTS SAVING AT 20	STARTS SAVING AT 30
2003–2012	$1,000 per year	—
2013–2022	—	$1,000 per year
2023–2032	—	$1,000 per year
2033–2042	—	$1,000 per year
2043–2047	—	$1,000 per year
Total at age 65	$157,843	$147,913

Assumes hypothetical annual return of 7 percent and no withdrawals.

How does this happen? Time and compounding! Compounding is like a bike coasting downhill; the farther it goes, the faster it goes.

To illustrate the power of compounding, ask yourself the age-old question: Would you rather have $10,000 right now or receive the total amount of a penny doubled each day at the end of a month? Most people go for the $10,000 up front. But if you double a penny every day—two cents the second day, four cents on the third, eight cents on the fourth, and so on—you end up with more than $10 million at the end of the month. Of course, normal compounding isn't going to double your money every day. But the longer compounding has to work its magic on your savings, the more power it has. And the less money you'll have to save to achieve your financial goals.

The Rule of 72

Speaking of doubling, the Rule of 72 can be used to determine approximately how many years it will take for your savings to double. Just divide 72 by the rate of return on your savings times 100. Assuming the rate of return on your investment is 7 percent, your savings will double in approximately ten years $(72/(.07 \times 100) = 10.3$ years).

THE CHALLENGE

January was a good month for Betsy. That was when the twenty-eight-year-old history teacher made the final payment on her student loan *and* her final car payment. "I felt such a sense of relief. Now, I don't owe anyone anything," Betsy explained. For a few months, Betsy used the money that had been going to loan payments to finish furnishing her apartment and to buy a better television. Then, Betsy's good financial feeling began to evaporate. "I didn't owe anything, but I hadn't saved anything either," she said. Betsy's passion is foreign travel and she dreams of retiring in her fifties when she will still be young enough for some heavy-duty adventure travel. In the meantime, she wants to use her summer vacations for lengthy trips abroad.

"I was feeling a little depressed," said Betsy. "My ambitious retirement and travel plans didn't mesh with my teacher's salary and my nonexistent savings."

THE PLAN

Betsy took advantage of an opportunity to visit a financial planner for a free consultation. "I felt a little silly because I didn't have any money," she said. "But my advisor made me feel comfortable right away." First, the advisor congratulated Betsy on becoming debt-free and resisting the temptation to incur credit card debt. Then she suggested they work together to create a financial plan that could help Betsy realize her dream of becoming a world traveler.

"The two things we agreed on first was that I needed a bank account with $3,000 savings as an emergency fund and that I should enroll immediately in my school district's 403(b) retirement plan." Under the 403(b) plan, money is automatically taken from Betsy's salary and placed in a tax-sheltered annuity. The money she contributes to the plan is tax-deferred, and so are the plan's earnings. "So I reduce my tax burden, and at the same time, have automatic savings, so I'm not tempted to spend the money," explained Betsy.

In addition to these steps, Betsy and the advisor discussed ways she could earn even more such as taking a summer job or returning to school to earn an administrator's degree.

"These are just the first steps," said Betsy. "I plan to keep working with my advisor over the next few years to set up an investment portfolio that will eventually give me the resources to fulfill my travel dreams."

Recovering Lost Savings

The savings discipline also means reducing nonessential expenses. Most consumers spend money on a lot of little things that are insignificant in themselves, but that add up to a major monetary drain. Learn to distinguish between "wants" and "needs." Do you absolutely "need" it? Or is the truth that you really just "want" it?

Everyone has different savings weaknesses, but here are a few common areas where people spend needlessly—or spend more than they should based on their level of income and savings.

The cost of raising a baby to adulthood averages more than $160,000.

Dining Out—There's nothing like going out for dinner. Good food, no cooking, no dishes. But the expense can add up fast. Meals prepared at home can be much less expensive.

- **Schedule when you'll dine out, and don't do it on the spur of the moment.**
- **Most restaurants serve meals that are too large for most of us to eat at one time.** Divide your meal in half and have it put it a to-go box at the start of the meal, or share a meal.
- **When dining out, drink ice water.** By not paying for soft drinks, coffee, wine, and cocktails, you can save a lot over the course of a year.
- **Watch the newspaper and mail for two-for-one deals or other specials.**

New Car—You lose thousands of dollars in value the minute you drive a new car off the lot. Slightly used cars can be a much better value for someone who wants to save money.

- **Give up the notion that you must have a new car every few years.** If your friends or neighbors are "keeping up with the Joneses," maybe you can purchase their "old car."
- **Wait until the new model is on the lot.** Then buy the previous year's model. The dealer will want to move the "old" model and you'll get a good deal.

smart step

If available, consider using an employer-provided child care and/or medical expense reimbursement plan to pay for these expenses.

Phone Bills—Excessive wireless phone use can add up. So can overuse of long distance calling. Consider e-mail as a substitute for some of those calls. Or, you could even write a letter.

Newspapers and Subscriptions—Drop unnecessary subscriptions. If you're stacking the reading material unread on the floor, it's time to reconsider.

Electronics—Electronic toys are fun, but if you need to save, cut back on the stereos, computer gadgets, CDs, DVDs, video games, wide screen televisions, and other electronic wonders. You don't have to be the first one in the neighborhood to purchase the newest toy. You know the prices will come down, so be patient.

Clothing—This is an area where you could save barrels of money.
- **Check out the consignment shops.** You can find amazing bargains on the clothes someone else wore only once or twice. Go for classic styles that don't go out of fashion.
- **Learn to accessorize.** There are many ways to make an "old" outfit look brand new.
- **Suggest a clothes exchange to friends or neighbors.** The item that you've left hanging in your closet since you bought it might be perfect for a friend, and vice versa.
- **Stay away from trendy fashions.**
- **Buy wash-and-wear clothes vs. dry-clean items.**

Cigarettes—If not for your health, consider giving up smoking for your budget. Remember, a pack a day adds up to well over $1,000 a year.

Coupons—Use coupons at the grocery store. Clipping coupons can add up to big savings over the long term.

Vacations—Vacations are an enjoyable part of life, but there are different levels of luxury from which to choose. If you need to save money, you can cut back on your travel expenditures.

- **Shop for bargains.** Visit reputable travel Web sites and sign up for e-mails alerting you to last-minute deals.
- **Drive instead of fly (or take the bus or train).**
- **Stay closer to home.** Visit all the places in your state that you've said you've always wanted to see. Some states offer special deals for residents during the off-season.

Finding Ways to Save

Here is a list of other ways to jump-start your savings plan:

- **Set up an investment plan at the bank or through a mutual fund or retirement account that automatically deducts a predetermined amount from your checking account each month.** After a while, you won't notice the deductions, but you will notice the steady buildup of your savings.
- **Transfer $5 or $10 to your savings account every time you hit the ATM.** When you spend, you also save; some money for now, some money for later.
- **When shopping, stick to a list.** Impulse bargains are no bargain if they end up costing you what you really want. A few exceptions: Sometimes you can save on holiday presents if you get them on sale and stash them away. Or if canned tuna isn't on your grocery list, but the store is selling it at a terrific price, go ahead and buy a few cans, assuming you regularly eat canned tuna.
- **Use what you've already paid for, such as the library or free concerts sponsored by your community.** Think of the money you save as a rebate on your local taxes. Read books, magazines, and newspapers, or borrow videos, tapes, and DVDs from the library instead of buying or renting.
- **Treat any interest as "found savings."** Reinvest it.

smart step

Start Now!

Calculate the growth of your savings.

Log on to
hrblock.com/advisor

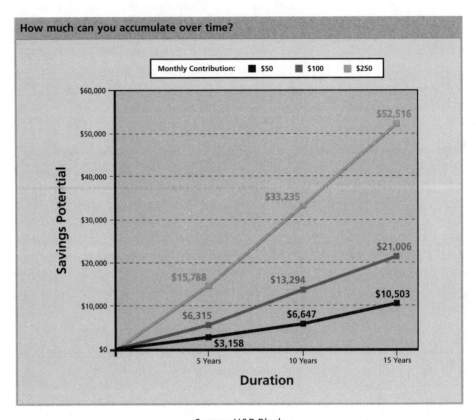

How much can you accumulate over time?

Monthly Contribution: ■ $50 ■ $100 ▨ $250

Savings Potential

$60,000
$50,000
$40,000
$30,000
$20,000
$10,000
$0

$52,516
$33,235
$21,006
$15,788
$13,294
$10,503
$6,315
$6,647
$3,158

5 Years   10 Years   15 Years

Duration

Source: H&R Block

This chart assumes a 2.0% growth rate, compounded monthly and is for illustrative purposes only. Your actual rate of return may vary.

■ **Have breakfast at home and pack a lunch.**
■ **Buy the store brand or generic brand.** Instead of buying the national brand, you may find there is no difference at all in the quality, but what a savings! If you must buy the national brand, become a coupon clipper.
■ **If you buy large quantities, consider joining a wholesale club.** Make sure you are getting a good buy and not just a larger quantity.
■ **Sell your unneeded items.** You might be able to cut the clutter in your base-

ment and bolster your savings by having a garage sale or taking items to a consignment shop.

- **Take another look at your debts.** See if there's a way to refinance so that you're paying less interest. Put the difference into your savings.

If you've tried everything, but still can't come up with the extra money for a savings plan, you have one other option—get a better job (or get a second job). Seriously. Many people struggle to meet expenses for years, wondering why they can't make ends meet and can't save money. The answer is simple: They need to make more money. Many good workers settle for low-paying jobs, and stay in those jobs for years instead of looking for better jobs paying better money.

Saving Checklist

How much should you have in your savings account? That depends on your financial needs and goals. In addition to an emergency fund that will cover your expenses for at least three to six months if you lose your job, you might want to set up savings funds for several other reasons.

✓ ➤ **Here are several options**

- A **retirement fund**
- A **car fund** for insurance, repairs, and saving for a new car
- A **vacation fund** that will enable you to pay cash for pleasure travel
- A **special events fund** that can be used for special occasions such as birthdays, anniversaries, holidays, and other special events
- An **insurance fund** that will cover such things as long-term care insurance or insurance for a family member
- A **medical fund** to handle health club memberships, routine annual exams and expenses, or emergencies

smart step

If you can't meet a minimum balance requirement for an investment account, consider having money automatically transferred every month from your checking account. Doing so often lowers the required deposit.

The two most important things to remember about saving are to start right away and keep at it. Use your long-range financial goals as motivation to save more and spend less. The miracle of compounding plus your discipline in sticking to your savings plan will pay huge future dividends.

the ESSENTIALS

1 To make the most of the money you have, put it to work sooner. The earlier you do, the more time it has to increase its value.

2 Look for hidden savings by becoming a smart spender and smart saver. Small amounts can add up quickly over time.

3 A savings discipline means cutting out nonessential expenses in your spending habits.

4 The more you cut your expenses, the more you can save.

5 Make specific savings goals for various purposes, and meet them.

6 [**INSURANCE BASICS:**

Buying Insurance on You
and Your Belongings]

"It's not whether you get knocked down, it's
whether you get up."

—Vince Lombardi

smart step

Always be sure you understand when your insurance coverage becomes effective.

It has been said that nothing is certain in life but death and taxes. If that is true, then there's a lot of uncertainty left. For example you don't know if and when you'll be in an accident, get sick, and, generally, you don't know when you're going to die.

With all that uncertainty surrounding you and your family, you can decide to accept the financial consequences of future risks or you can minimize your potential losses by sharing the risks with an insurance company—or by transferring them completely. That's what insurance is all about—managing risk.

There's nothing magical about insurance. Insurance can't save your life or keep your car on the road, it can't stop your home from catching fire, and it can't safeguard you from sickness or injury. But it can protect you and your family from the high financial costs associated with all of those calamities.

That's why everyone needs insurance—to keep life's inevitable emergencies from becoming financial disasters. If you're properly insured, you and your family can get knocked down and get back up again without having to worry about the financial consequences. When you start thinking about what type of insurance you need, remember that there are two fundamental categories of insurance coverage:

- Insurance on the things you own (such as property or liability)
- Insurance on you (such as life, health, and disability)

How much insurance do you need? It depends on what other resources you have to provide an income if you can't work, or to repair damages to the home, or to pay medical bills—and still pay your mortgage and put food on the table. If you want to protect yourself and your assets, you probably won't want to assume all of the risks yourself.

Insuring Your Belongings

Balancing paying insurance premiums against the possibility for disaster doesn't have to be a guessing game. Once you get the facts about the types and levels of coverage that are available, you can make an informed decision about what is right for you. When insuring your belongings—such as a home, car, and personal property—look not just at what you paid for something, but also at what you would need to pay to replace or repair it. When reviewing your options, you'll also want to focus on removing or reducing the risks associated with the big calamities. Insuring against the small losses you can handle on your own can sometimes be a waste of money.

You want to make sure that your insurance coverage takes care of the big financial losses you can't handle on your own. By increasing your **deductible** (the amount you'll pay in the event of a covered loss), you can reduce the cost of coverage. But don't underinsure the important things. For instance, you need enough coverage on your home to buy or rebuild an equivalent home should something unfortunate occur.

Two key possessions you probably need to consider insuring are your automobile and your home.

Automobile—In most states, you're required to have automobile insurance. It is something you definitely need if you drive and you could face a fine and possibly suspension of your license if you don't carry it. The liability part of a personal auto policy covers two basic types of damage that could result from an accident: bodily injury and property damage. You could be held liable for either or both types of damage. Most states require a minimum amount of liability insurance. The bodily injury portion provides coverage for a legal obligation as a result of the injury or death of another person. The property damage portion provides coverage when your vehicle damages someone else's property such as a car, building, or fence.

Your automobile insurance policy could also include coverage for a variety of other risks, including:

- the cost of medical services for you and others in your vehicle;
- protection for your vehicle from losses such as fire, theft, or hail;
- coverage for the damage to your vehicle from a collision with another vehicle or object; and
- protection for you if the driver of another vehicle does not have insurance coverage or does not have enough insurance coverage to pay for your injuries.

There is a wide variety of other coverage available that can be added to your policy (such as towing or rental reimbursement if your vehicle is being repaired from a covered claim) and you'll need to determine which ones are important to you.

If you want better rates, you could buy a vehicle with a good safety rating or one that isn't a favorite target of thieves. Most insurance companies often offer reduced rates for safer vehicles. You should also check with your insurance professional to determine how much you might be able to save by increasing your deductible. And, of course, if you drive safely, avoiding accidents and speeding tickets, that can help keep your rates lower as well.

Home—If you own your home, homeowners insurance is an absolute must because you can be exposed to a wide variety of risks to your home and its contents such as fire, storms, and burglary, and because your mortgage lender will require it. And don't forget personal liability. Someone may get hurt on your property, or your dog may bite someone, and you could be liable for the person's injuries. You'll want to have adequate coverage on your home, your personal property, and for your personal liability. So purchase enough coverage to repair or replace your home, all of your possessions, and to protect yourself from losing everything in a lawsuit.

If you rent your home, you don't have to worry about the cost of replacing the building. That's up to your landlord. But you do need to get a policy on your possessions. Renter's insurance is generally inexpensive and often overlooked until a calamity occurs.

When It Rains, It Pours—Do You Need an Umbrella?

So you've covered all of your bases by purchasing insurance coverage for claims you may become liable for, but will it be enough? With today's skyrocketing liability costs, how can you be sure? Say, for example, you are in an automobile accident and are liable for damages that are in excess of the limits of your policy. Do you have other assets (such as your savings account) you'd like to use to pay for the damages? If not, you may want to help protect the rest of your assets in case of a large claim that exceeds the limits of your policy by purchasing umbrella coverage. Umbrella coverage provides just what the name implies: coverage over your other policies. It kicks in after the basic liability of the other polices it covers has been exhausted and usually has a limit of $1 million or more. This coverage is added on top of the limit for other policies it covers (such as automobile or homeowners). Best of all, this large amount of coverage can be relatively inexpensive to acquire. See your insurance professional for more information.

Insurance companies may reward you for making smart decisions. Look into discounts for installing safety features in both your car and home—items such as airbags, anti-lock brakes, and security systems. You may also be able to get discounts for not smoking, being a good student, being a senior citizen, or for driving a limited number of miles per year. And most insurers will give you a

smart step

If you're thinking about having a baby, line up health insurance well in advance. Many individual policies limit pregnancy coverage.

discount if you have multiple policies with them. Not only will it be more convenient for you, but it will also be easier for your insurance professional to identify any potential gaps or overlaps in your coverage.

When considering what coverage to purchase, don't forget about other vehicles (such as motorcycles, boats, and ATVs) and dwellings (such as your vacation or rental property). Remember, you'll want to make sure that you are covered in the event of a calamity. It is easy to overlook items that should be covered, so be sure to discuss all of the options you have for coverage with your insurance professional.

Getting Medical Coverage

Health insurance is one of the most important types of coverage. Without it, a serious illness or a major operation could wipe out your entire life savings and put you hopelessly in debt. And unlike auto insurance—something that some fortunate policyholders may never have to use—health insurance is something virtually every person and every family needs from time to time.

Health insurance can help you stave off financial disaster, but it isn't inexpensive. If you have coverage through your place of employment, that can be a huge benefit. Most employers require employees to contribute a portion of their salary to help cover the cost. Some policies also often require a deductible to be paid for medical visits and filling prescriptions. But even with the extra costs, an employee health insurance plan can be well worth the money. Just ask anyone who has to pay health insurance entirely out of his or her own pocket.

HMO, PPO, or Traditional Insurance

I f you have health insurance, you probably have traditional health insurance or participate in a HMO (Health Maintenance Organization) or PPO (Preferred Provider Organization). With traditional health insurance, you may pay a little more, but you may also have a wider choice of the doctors, clinics, and hospitals you may use and may avoid having to get approval from a "primary care physician" or "gatekeeper" first. You will usually have to spend a certain amount (a deductible) on medical bills each year before your insurance starts to pay. After that, you will have to pay either a co-payment, which is a stated amount of the bill, such as $15, or a percentage of the bill such as 20 or 30 percent called co-insurance. The insurance company will pay the rest of the charge based on what it considers reasonable and customary. If you already see a doctor you trust, check to see if he or she participates in the insurance plan you want; if not, you'll have to decide whether you're willing to trade your existing doctor for lower **premiums**.

HMOs were originally introduced as a way to save money on health coverage—if you were willing to accept some tradeoffs. Those tradeoffs include going only to the select physicians, clinics, and hospitals that are members of your HMO, but also include payment of 100 percent of covered expenses (no-deductible plans) and no claim forms to file.

A PPO is generally less flexible than traditional health insurance plans but more flexible than an HMO. You can see any health care provider you want (including a specialist), but your co-payment will be higher if the physician you choose is not a "preferred provider"—a physician with whom the health plan has a contract. PPOs will almost always require that you get their approval before entering

plain talk

Premiums are periodic payments by the insured to an insurance company in exchange for insurance coverage.

a hospital. But they are more likely to fully cover checkups and other preventive medical services than traditional health insurance plans, and most preferred providers will file your claims for you.

Each type of insurance offers a broad range of coverage options. For instance, some charge a $15 co-payment for all doctor's visits, and a higher co-payment for a hospital stay. Some cover chiropractic care, others don't. Some charge a low deductible, but a higher premium. Other policies lower your premiums, but charge a deductible on hospital stays that cost $1,000 or more. Some policies cover prescriptions or dental care, others don't. It's up to you to choose the options and the deductible level that are right for you.

When shopping for insurance, it pays to ask your insurance professional or benefits administrator a lot of questions to determine which plan will best meet your needs and is the best value for you or your family. Also, if both you and your spouse work, make sure you're not paying for overlapping health care coverage through both employers' plans.

Disability Insurance

What's your most valuable asset? If you said your home, you're wrong. If you said your car, you're wrong. For most people, it's their ability to earn a living. If you own a $200,000 home and earn $50,000 a year, you'll earn far more over your lifetime than the value of the home—unless something happens that leaves you unable to work.

Your chances of becoming disabled are probably greater than you think. Over the course of your career, you are several times more likely to be injured than to die. Advances in medical technology mean that you may now survive a disease or accident that might have killed you several years ago. However, if you're disabled, you will still need an income in addition to coverage for your medical costs. Health insurance won't keep food on the table.

That's where disability insurance can help ease the financial strain. It won't replace your normal income, but it will help pay the bills while you recover. So, if you think that Social Security will pay these disability benefits, you should know that Social Security denies coverage more than it awards benefits. And even if you are eligible, coverage doesn't start for five months, and it covers only disabilities that are expected to last at least a year and/or result in death. Worker's compensation covers you only for on-the-job injuries, and employer-provided disability coverage is lost if you change jobs.

If you have a job, your company may already provide disability coverage. But if you're self-employed or you work for a firm that provides no coverage, disability insurance should be an essential part of your insurance coverage.

The drawback to disability insurance is that it can be fairly expensive when compared to other types of insurance such as health and life insurance—and you may never use it. But if you ever do need it, it can make a huge difference in your life and your ability to support yourself and your family. One way to help reduce the cost of disability insurance is to agree to wait a greater amount of time before receiving benefits when you're disabled. This is called the **elimination period**. The quicker your benefits start, the more you'll pay in premiums.

Here are some things to look for in a disability policy:

- **Get a policy that is both noncancelable and is guaranteed renewable.**
  This provision guarantees that the policy can't be canceled and the premiums can't be raised for the life of the policy as long as you continue to pay your premiums. A guaranteed renewable policy is one that can't be canceled as long as you pay your premiums, but the premium could be raised under certain

plain talk

The elimination period is the "waiting period" between events in a policy, such as between the time when a disability occurs and the time the first benefit is paid.

circumstances (the circumstances must be approved by the state department of insurance).

- **You also may want to consider a policy that adjusts the benefit each year based on the cost of living.** That will help ensure that your benefits in 2020 will go as far as they did in 2003.
- **If possible, purchase disability insurance through a group.** That will help lower the cost of the premiums.

Here's a worksheet that will help you determine how much replacement income you would need in the event you become disabled.

DISABILITY INSURANCE WORKSHEET

1 | **Monthly income needed:** | _____

2 | **Estimated income sources:**

Monthly Social Security
disability benefits* (not
available for first 5 months
of disability)   _____

Income from savings   _____

Other income (spouse, etc.)   _____

3 | **Subtotal all estimated income sources:** | _____

4 | **Subtract Line 3 from Line 1 to get income needed from insurance:** | _____

*Go to www.ssa.gov to get an estimate or refer to the annual statement you receive a few months before your birthday.

Life Insurance

When you've coasted to a stop on the side of the road because you're out of gas, what you need from a passing stranger is enough gas to get to the nearest station. In a similar way, what you need from life insurance is enough to get your spouse and/or dependents to the next source of income, whatever that might be: Social Security, income from investments, a pension, the children's own salary after they're out of school.

Life insurance is not intended to be a lottery ticket, leaving your spouse or family with millions in the bank. For most people, the main purpose of life insurance is to replace their income to provide enough money for their dependents. Other uses of life insurance include paying off the debts of the deceased and creating an estate for the heirs. Even if you're single and you have no children or other dependents, you might need life insurance coverage for reasons such as these.

There are two main types of life insurance, *term* and *whole life*. Put simply, term life insurance provides death-benefit protection for a specified period of time, while whole life policies provide a lifetime death benefit as well as a savings account. If you're looking for coverage for a short period of time, term life insurance may make sense.

Term life insurance can provide good value for your dollar. Term life insurance is relatively inexpensive (when compared with whole life insurance) and it provides an insured's survivors with a benefit upon the insured's death, but it has no value while the insured is still alive. On the other hand, while a whole life policy will cost more initially than a term policy (for the same amount of coverage), it does build up a cash balance that you can borrow against, cash in while you're alive, or have added to the death benefit.

Before you select an insurance policy, spend some time with your insurance professional to determine which type of policy best meets your needs.

fast fact

Life insurance proceeds paid as a death benefit to a named beneficiary are received free from federal income tax.

Term life insurance is a type of life insurance policy that provides protection for a specified period. If you die while the policy is in force, your beneficiary receives the amount of insurance.

TERM LIFE INSURANCE

SELLING POINTS	THINGS TO THINK ABOUT
Premiums can be lower than for whole life insurance.	As you get older, buying term insurance will get more expensive, possibly prohibitively expensive.
You can generally afford more coverage.	Your beneficiaries benefit only if you die while the policy is in force.
Some policies are renewable without a physical exam, but premiums increase significantly.	Unless your policy is renewable, coverage can become more difficult to get as you get older.
Some policies can be converted to whole life insurance.	It may not make sense to convert the entire policy benefit.
It's more straightforward and easier to understand.	Its function is limited to providing only a death benefit.

Life Insurance Checklist

Working with your insurance professional, you'll want to determine the appropriate amount of life insurance you'll need. You'll need to consider a number of factors, which will vary depending on your own personal circumstances. Here are some of the factors you'll want to consider:

- ☐ **A reasonable estimate of annual living expenses**
- ☐ **Burial costs and other final expenses**
- ☐ **Capital preservation or liquidation** (does the beneficiary want to live off the income the life insurance proceeds can produce or does he or she intend to spend it?)
- ☐ **College education expenses for dependents**
- ☐ **Debts of the insured such as credit cards and loans**
- ☐ **Emergency fund**

WHOLE LIFE INSURANCE	
SELLING POINTS	**THINGS TO THINK ABOUT**
The cash value of your policy grows tax-deferred.	The taxes on any income earned by the policy generally are due when you withdraw it. Proceeds up to your cost basis (the amount you contributed) are received tax free, the excess is taxable.
You may be able to obtain a policy loan against the cash value of the policy.	Any outstanding loan will be deducted from the death benefit if it is not repaid.
You may not be able to get life insurance later, or else it will be very expensive.	You may not always have people who depend on you for the income that life insurance is supposed to replace, or have other needs for life insurance, such as debt repayment.
You're getting something in addition to the death benefit protection for your premium payments—for example, you can borrow against the cash value.	The interest rate you're quoted may not always stay the same, depending on the type of policy—most do have a guaranteed rate of return.
It's a way to save automatically.	There are many ways to save automatically, some of which may have better returns than your life insurance contract.
Variation among policies offers flexibility to tailor premiums and death benefits to meet your needs.	Numerous options make comparison shopping more difficult than with term insurance.

plain talk

Whole life insurance is a type of life insurance that combines insurance protection with a savings feature and is intended to be held for the lifetime of the insured. It treats part of your premiums as an investment (the policy's "cash value").

- [ ] Estate administration expenses such as probate fees and taxes
- [ ] Existing life insurance policies
- [ ] Insured's earnings for the period of time that income replacement would be needed, including anticipated future salary increases
- [ ] Likelihood the surviving spouse will remarry
- [ ] Length of time the children should be provided for
- [ ] Other sources of income such as pension plans, IRAs, etc.
- [ ] Work future of the surviving spouse

THE CHALLENGE

Ray has two young daughters, ages five and four months. While he is in great health and has a lucrative job in the publishing industry, he is concerned about what would happen financially to his wife and children if something should happen to him. Since his wife has chosen to stay at home while the children are young, he wonders where the income would come from to provide his family financial support in the short term, and where the money would come from for his daughters to be able to attend college in the future.

Ray has some whole life insurance that he purchased a few years ago, and participates in the group term insurance that is offered through his employer, but he doesn't know if it is enough to take care of his family. His employer's enrollment period for benefits is coming up soon, and he wonders if he should take advantage of any more of the group term life insurance that is available, or purchase another policy from his insurance professional.

THE PLAN

Ray makes an appointment with Roger, his insurance professional, someone whom he has trusted with his insurance protection for many years. After looking carefully at the future financial needs that Ray's family may have and the many options that he has for purchasing additional life insurance protection, Roger suggests the following plan that utilizes a mixture of whole life and term life protection to meet Ray's family's future needs.

Roger suggests keeping the whole life policy in force that Ray has been funding for the last several years. This policy has built up a nice cash value, against which Ray could borrow in the future, if necessary. Secondly, he suggests that Ray continue to participate in his employer's group term life insurance plan, as it also allows him to purchase supplemental group term life insurance on his wife in case something should happen to her. If something were to happen to her, Ray would need additional funds to cover other expenses such as child care that is now being provided by his wife. Finally, Roger recommends that Ray purchase an amount of term life insurance that is equal to the difference between the financial needs that have been identified (short-term income and future college expenses) and the amount of insurance that he already has in place.

After reviewing all of these options, Ray is convinced that this is the right plan for him. "While I may not like having to pay for something I may never need to use, I sure can sleep better knowing that my family will be taken care of financially if something happens to me," Ray said.

Long-Term Care Insurance

For many people today, long-term care has become one of their most financially critical issues. Typically, we spend thirty to forty years saving for retirement and never consider that the high cost of long-term care might totally wipe out our nest egg long before we die.

Who would take care of you if you had a stroke? Would your husband quit his job? Would your parent be physically able to do it? On the other hand, who would take care of your mother if she were in a terrible accident? Would you be able to add this to the roles you're already playing? And how would the additional financial costs be covered?

If you think long-term care is needed only for the elderly, think again. While a slight majority of people in need of long-term care are over age sixty-five, working-age adults (ages eighteen to sixty-four) come in a close second. The bottom line is that a person of any age may find himself or herself in need of long-term care.

Now that we have your attention, let's look at what long-term care means. Long-term care is the type of care that you may need if you can no longer perform daily living activities by yourself, such as bathing, eating, or getting dressed. It also includes care that you would need if you had a long-term disease such as Alzheimer's. Care can be received in a variety of settings: your own home, assisted living facilities, nursing homes, adult day care centers, or hospice facilities.

Long-term care can be covered completely or in part by long-term care insurance. Most plans let you choose the amount of the coverage you want, as well as how and where you want to use your benefits. A comprehensive plan includes benefits for all levels of care—custodial to skilled.

fast fact

As people age, the chances of needing long-term care increases significantly.

Designed to cover extended stays in hospital-type facilities, long-term care policies typically provide a certain amount of coverage for each day, week, or month you require care. That figure, along with your age and how long you're willing to wait until benefits start, determines the cost of the policy.

Long-term care (LTC) insurance will help you protect your assets in case of a long-term illness or disability by paying benefits if the injured or ill person is unable to function independently. If you don't buy LTC insurance and end up needing it, the alternatives can be pretty grim. You could use up all the assets that you worked your entire life to acquire. You can't depend on Medicare because it doesn't pay for most nursing or home care. Medicaid is the largest source of public money, paying almost half of the nation's nursing home care. To qualify for Medicaid, you must "spend down" your assets. Long-term care insurance can help preserve your wealth and keep you off Medicaid.

Long-term care policies can be purchased from ages eighteen to eighty-five, but the sooner you buy it, the less it will cost over time. Why? Because the premium is based on your current age. If you are convinced of the benefits of long-term care insurance, consult with your insurance professional and make sure you understand all the provisions of the policy and all of your options for purchasing coverage before you actually buy.

Medicare, Medicaid, and Medigap Insurance

When you're counting down to your sixty-fifth birthday, there are two decisions you will need to make about Medicare coverage: whether to sign up for Medicare Part B coverage, and what type of Medicare plan suits you best.

Medicare Part A is basically hospital insurance. It includes hospital care, skilled nursing care, certain types of home health care, and hospice care. Part B is medical insurance that covers doctors' bills, lab fees, home health care such as physical therapy, and outpatient hospital services.

To qualify for Part A, you will need to sign up by age sixty-five, unless you're already collecting Social Security benefits before then, in which case you're automatically enrolled in both Parts A and B. You can postpone signing up for Medicare B, but if you do, you'll have to wait until the next rollover period to enroll.

If you're already covered by your company or union plan, check to see what happens to your coverage at age sixty-five, when you become eligible for Medicare. Many plans cover only what Medicare Part B doesn't cover. Also, your cost for Part B is increased 10 percent for every year you wait to sign up after age sixty-five. The one exception is if you sign up while you're still insured by your employer's plan or shortly after it ends.

If you have both Parts A and B, you also have to choose which type of plan you want: Original Medicare or Medicare + Choice. The *Medicare Personal Plan Finder*, an interactive tool available at www.medicare.gov can help you sort through the choices. Or you can call 800-MEDICARE (800-633-4227) to get more information mailed to you.

Medicaid—Medicaid provides health care coverage for people below a specified income level. Each state has its own eligibility requirements; if you think you might qualify, check with your state medical assistance office to see if you're eligible.

smart step

Consider your needs for life, long-term care, and medical insurance when planning your retirement strategy.

smart step

Consult with your tax professional before purchasing a long-term care policy. Benefits from policies that meet certain IRS requirements may be tax-free.

Supplemental (Medigap) Insurance—Medigap policies cover what Medicare doesn't, such as deductibles and co-payments. In most states, ten different standard types of policies are available. Lettered A through J, they offer different menus of coverage and sometimes require that you use specified hospitals and doctors. For more information about buying a Medigap policy, use *Medigap Compare* an interactive tool available at www.medicare.gov or request a copy of the *Guide to Health Insurance for People with Medicare: Choosing a Medigap Policy* (CMS Publication Number 02110) from Medicare.

Shopping for Insurance

Over the course of your life, you will spend thousands of dollars on insurance. By all means, do some comparison shopping before you buy. There can be huge differences in premiums for the same coverage from one company to another.

Before you buy, compare prices from the most reputable insurance companies. You may also be able to get some quotes on the Internet to compare with the prices you get from a local insurance professional. You may well find that the Internet sites offer some lower rates. However, you need to weigh the cost savings of an Internet carrier against the personal relationship and service you would have with an insurance professional. Having a professional that understands your personal situation and that you can call in times of need can make your life much easier.

When discussing insurance options with an insurance professional—whether it's life, health, disability, or property—you may find the terms confusing. Make sure you understand exactly what you're buying and what you're paying for—now and in the future. If you're not sure of the terms of the coverage, ask him or her to explain it again—and again, if necessary. The insurance professional's job is to make sure you get the coverage that you need and understand exactly what you are buying.

the ESSENTIALS

1

Insurance can't protect you from life's calamities, but it can reduce or eliminate the associated financial costs.

2

Consider purchasing insurance coverage to replace the things (such as your possessions and your income) that you cannot afford to replace with your other assets.

3

When purchasing life insurance, there are many options to consider. Always keep in mind the basic purpose for which you are purchasing it, such as income replacement or to repay debts. Remember, even people without dependents may need life insurance.

4

Disability insurance covers your biggest financial asset: your ongoing ability to earn a living.

5

Don't automatically choose the least (or most) expensive health insurance; tailor coverage to your specific health care needs. Also, remember to insure the basics, such as your automobile and home, and consider an umbrella policy for added liability coverage.

6

Regardless of which Medicare options you choose, sign up for them three months or so before your sixty-fifth birthday. You'll need to decide whether to take both parts of Medicare—A (hospitalization) and B (medical care). You'll also have to decide whether you want original Medicare, managed care, or private fee-for-service.

smart step

Don't overlook life insurance coverage for a non-working spouse when you have children. If something were to happen to that spouse, you would probably incur new expenses such as child care services that were previously provided by that spouse.

7 [NESTING BEHAVIOR:
Buying and Maintaining a Home]

"Be it ever so humble, there's no place like home."
—J. Howard Payne

A home is much more than a roof over your head. It's an investment and a source of clout with lenders. If you need a loan, your home could provide **equity** and security, both of which lenders appreciate. Yes, a home keeps the rain off your head, but it also provides other great benefits.

A home can be thought of as an automatic savings plan. As you make mortgage payments, you're building equity for yourself rather than for a landlord. It also can be a source of great tax deductions. Generally, you can usually deduct all the interest you pay on your home mortgage as an itemized deduction. The same is true for the real estate taxes you pay. You can also use the value of your home to create greater personal wealth in other ways, perhaps by borrowing against the equity or renting it to generate income. Finally, a home can be an inflation-fighter because the value of your home often rises faster than inflation. In fact, if you have a fixed-rate mortgage, your housing costs as a percentage of your income should actually decrease over time.

There's another advantage of owning your own home. When you sell your home, up to $250,000 of your gain ($500,000 if you file jointly with your spouse) is generally tax-free. You need to meet certain conditions, so discuss the sale of your home with your tax professional *before* selling.

Buy or Rent?

Even with all the advantages of home ownership, not everyone is ready to buy a home. If you answer *yes* to the following questions, you may be ready to consider buying a home.

■ **Do you plan to live in the same area for several more years?** If you expect to move to another city within the next couple of years, renting may be a better option. It could cost you more to buy and sell the home than you would gain from ownership.

- **Do you have a steady income that will enable you to keep up the payments for the next fifteen to thirty years?** If you don't expect to work steadily for the foreseeable future, you may not be ready for a home yet.

- **Do you have the extra time and money to put into maintaining a home?** Keeping the grass mowed, the hedges trimmed, the roof from leaking, the toilets working, and the dozens of other odd jobs that go with home ownership can take a toll on your time and pocketbook. Owning a home is a big commitment.

- **Do you have the money to cover the down payment?** The amount required to make a down payment depends on the lender. Some lenders require a down payment as low as 3 percent, and in some cases no down payment may be required. Also be sure to consider the amount you'll need for closing costs, such as points and other fees. Also keep in mind that if your down payment is less than 20 percent, you may have to pay **private mortgage insurance** (PMI) each month.

- **Do you have a credit rating solid enough to qualify for a mortgage?** If you're unsure about your credit history, check out your credit report and do whatever is necessary to bring your credit rating up to par.

If you answered *yes* to all five questions, then you're probably ready to consider buying a home. The sooner you buy, the sooner you can start enjoying all the advantages of home ownership.

plain talk

Private mortgage insurance (PMI) is insurance coverage that protects the lender if the buyer defaults on the loan.

**smart
step**

Start Now!

Calculate the
value of home
ownership.

Log on to
hrblock.com/advisor

How Much Home Can You Afford?

Several factors help determine the amount of home you can get for your money.

Your Income—The mortgage lender naturally will need to know what you currently earn and what you will likely be earning over the life of the loan.

Down Payment—The more money you can put down on a new home, the more expensive a home you can buy, or the lower your monthly payments will be. You also may be able to afford a home in a more desirable location.

Monthly Payments—How much can you afford to pay each month? The more you can come up with for your monthly mortgage payment, the more expensive a home you can afford. Traditionally, lenders have expected home buyers to pay no more than 28 percent of their gross monthly income toward mortgage payments, taxes, and insurance, although some lenders allow as much as 32 percent to go for these items.

Existing Debt—How much debt do you have already? The less, the better. When lenders decide how large a mortgage you qualify for, they look primarily at your ongoing ability to make your mortgage payments. Lenders use two formulas that help them determine that. First, they look at how much of your income your home payments will require (your housing ratio). Second, they look at how much of your income will be going to pay off all debt, including the mortgage, credit cards, car loans, etc. (your debt ratio). Lenders generally prefer that your total monthly debt payments account for no more than about 36 percent of your gross monthly income.

YOUR HOUSING RATIO

Your monthly home payments (Principal, Interest, Taxes, and Insurance, or PITI) divided by your gross monthly income equals your housing ratio.

PITI $_____ ÷ Monthly Income $_____ = _____ Your Housing Ratio

EXAMPLE:

Monthly payments (PITI):	**$1,100**
Monthly income:	**$4,000**
Your Housing Ratio:	.275

$1,100 ÷ $4,000 = .275 × 100 = 27.5%

YOUR DEBT RATIO

Monthly home payments (PITI) plus your monthly payments on other debt equals your total monthly debt payments. Your total monthly debt payments divided by your gross monthly income equals your debt ratio.

PITI $_____ + Other Monthly Debt Payments $_____ = $_____ Total Monthly Debt Payments

Total Monthly Debt Payments $_____ ÷ Monthly Income $_____ = _____ Your Debt Ratio

EXAMPLE:

Monthly payments (PITI):	**$1,100**
	+
Monthly payments on other debt:	**$ 700**
	=
Your total debt payments:	**$1,800**
	÷
Your monthly income:	**$4,000**
	=
Your Debt Ratio:	.45

$1,800 ÷ $4,000 = .45 × 100 = 45%

109

**smart
step**

When compar
ing mortgages,
compare all
terms of the
loan including
the length of
the loan, inter-
est rates, and
number of
points charged.

Interest Rate—The lower the prevailing interest rate, the more home you can afford. Interest rates can make a significant difference in your monthly payments. For instance, on a 30-year, $120,000 mortgage at 10 percent interest, you would pay about $1,050 per month, not including taxes and insurance. At 6 percent interest, you would pay only about $719 per month. Or, to put it another way, $1,050 a month would buy you a $175,000 home at 6 percent interest, but only a $120,000 home at 10 percent interest.

Length of the Loan—You can buy a bigger home if you're willing to take on a longer mortgage. Most mortgages are for fifteen, twenty, or thirty years. A 15-year mortgage is paid off more quickly—and with thousands of dollars less in interest charges—but the monthly payments are higher. You may not be able to afford the home you want on a 15-year mortgage, but it might work out with a 20- or 30-year mortgage.

The Neighborhood—Home prices vary considerably from one neighborhood to another. You may not be able to afford a home in your favorite neighborhood initially, but home prices in more desirable neighborhoods generally increase faster than in less desirable neighborhoods. Once you've built up some equity in the home you purchase, you may be able to sell it to generate a larger down payment for a home in a more desirable neighborhood.

Pre-Approval

Before you shop for a home, shop for a lender. This step can make it much easier to purchase the home you want. Once you find a lender that offers a good interest rate with acceptable terms, ask that lender to pre-approve you for a mortgage. You could be pre-approved over the telephone or online.

Pre-approval is basically the same process as final approval. You fill out some forms detailing your income, assets, and debts. The lender looks over your forms, reviews your credit history, and determines exactly how much they will approve for your loan.

Keep in mind that a pre-approval is not a commitment to lend—the loan officer who pre-approved you does not make the final approval. Nevertheless, once you're pre-approved, you can shop with confidence for the homes in your price range without wasting your time on homes that won't fit into your financial picture. You may have been given a pre-approval letter that you'll be able to show when you submit a bid for a home. With it, the seller is more likely to take your bid over one from somebody who has not already been pre-approved.

Finding Money for the Down Payment

The hardest part of buying a home for most people is coming up with the down payment. If you need a 20 percent down payment, that can be a considerable amount of money. On a $100,000 home that's $20,000, and on a $250,000 home, that's $50,000. It's difficult to save that kind of money—particularly while you're paying rent, buying a car, and raising a family.

fast fact

You may be able to borrow money for your down payment from your retirement plan at work. Contact your plan administrator to find out if this option is available to you and if so, whether you meet the requirements.

Make sure your credit report is accurate before you apply for a loan. You won't want to be turned down for a loan because of an error on your credit report.

Here's how some new homeowners have covered the down payment:

Parents—It's not unusual for new home buyers to get a portion of their down payment from parents or other relatives. If you are lucky enough to have your family help you out, good for you.

Inheritance—Have you inherited money from a parent or relative—or do you expect to? Put any inheritance away in an untouchable account, and use it to help with the down payment.

Federal Government—The federal government offers several programs designed to help new home buyers. Both the Federal Housing Administration (FHA) and the Department of Veterans Affairs (VA) offer loans that require little or no money down for first-time home buyers and veterans. Ask your lender if you qualify. Lenders administer the loans, so they'll know if you're eligible and how to apply. Also, the Rural Housing Service (RHS) offers low-interest loans to people who live in rural areas or small towns.

State Government—Some states offer help for first-timers. Again, lenders should be familiar with what's available for you.

Fannie Mae, Freddie Mac, and Ginnie Mae—Three corporations that were created by Congress can help you get a better mortgage. Fannie Mae (the Federal National Mortgage Association), Freddie Mac (the Federal Home Loan Mortgage Corporation), and Ginnie Mae (the Government National Mortgage Association) cater to people with low or moderate incomes. Although these corporations are not consumer direct lenders, qualified lenders can help you apply for loan products created by these organizations. If you qualify, it could mean not only a lower down payment but also a lower interest rate.

Investments—Some lenders will allow you to use your stocks and bonds as collateral to qualify for a home loan with less money up front.

Retirement Savings—Your retirement savings generally should not be touched for any reason other than retirement. A home can be such a great investment that you might consider tapping into your retirement fund to make it possible to buy one. If you have an IRA, you can withdraw up to $10,000 penalty-free to buy a first home. The amount you include in your income depends on whether the IRA is a Roth IRA or traditional IRA and, if a traditional IRA, whether you have made nondeductible contributions. Be sure to consult your tax professional before making a withdrawal to determine what taxes and penalties may apply.

Your lender should be able to guide you through the various options to find a down payment solution that is right for you. Remember, if you can't afford a 20 percent down payment, you may be required to buy private mortgage insurance, which serves as a guarantee to the lender that if you don't pay, the insurance company will pay for any loss (up to a certain point) experienced by the lender after foreclosure. Buying private mortgage insurance is expensive, and can add dramatically to the cost of paying for your home. But it does allow you to buy a home with as little as 3 to 5 percent up front.

Mortgage Strategies

There are several factors to consider when choosing a mortgage. When you're calculating the total cost of the home, don't forget the costs of taking out the loan, called closing costs. The more points you pay, generally the lower your interest rate. A rule of thumb is to equate each point with ¼ (.25) percent interest rate. If you pay an extra point on a 7 percent mortgage, that would lower your rate to about 6.75 percent. Is it worth it? That depends on how long you expect to stay in the home. If you plan to stay for many years, paying extra points up front might save you money in the long run, but if you expect to move to another home in just a few years, you generally

plain talk

A point is a fee for borrowing money equal to 1 percent of the amount you borrow and is paid at the time of the closing of the home. The more points you pay, the lower the interest rate.

An ARM can be tied to the rate on U.S. Treasury Bills, the London Inter-Bank Offer Rate (LIBOR), certificates of deposit, or another index. The mortgage lender links the ARM rate to the index, usually settling it at several percentage points above the index. When these rates go up or down, so does your mortgage interest rate and monthly payment.

FIXED-RATE MORTGAGE (FRM)

ADVANTAGES	DISADVANTAGES
▪ Rates and payments stay the same (even if interest rates increase). You can manage your money more easily because you know in advance what your mortgage payment will be. Your monthly mortgage payment may change a little from year to year, due to increased property taxes and insurance on your home, but the total cost of interest and principal will stay exactly the same each month for the entire 15, 20 or 30-year life of the loan. ▪ It is easy to understand.	▪ You can't take advantage of falling interest rates unless you refinance, which involves time and money (in the form of closing costs). ▪ It can be expensive if you're borrowing during a time of high interest rates. ▪ The mortgage can't be customized for you except in terms of length (15, 20, or 30-year.) An FRM is generally the same from lender to lender.

shouldn't pay the extra points. Your lender can help you determine whether paying extra points up front would be worthwhile for you.

Fixed-Rate Mortgage (FRM)—Fixed-rate mortgages are generally offered as 15- 20- or a 30-year mortgages. You will have the comfort of knowing exactly what your monthly mortgage payment will be, no matter how interest rates change in the future.

Adjustable-Rate Mortgage (ARM)—Adjustable-rate mortgages usually carry an interest rate that is somewhat lower than a fixed-rate mortgage. That could help lower your monthly payments. However, the lender is permitted to adjust the interest rate periodically as outlined in the terms of the loan, meaning your payments could change as interest rates change.

Balloon Mortgage—If you can't afford a big down payment, you might be able to get a balloon mortgage. With a balloon mortgage, you pay a little up

ADJUSTABLE-RATE MORTGAGE (ARM)

ADVANTAGES	DISADVANTAGES
■ Early in the loan, you'll have lower rates and payments than with an FRM.	■ The interest rate and your payment could rise over the life of the loan. There are **caps** to the increases, but your payment might increase significantly if interest rates rise significantly. The APR for an ARM is a moving target—because neither you nor the lender can predict what the interest rate will be in the future.
■ You may be able to purchase a larger home than you might with an FRM.	
■ Lenders can be flexible in determining the features of the loan, such as the caps and the adjustment index.	
■ If you're not planning on living in the home for very long, it offers a more economical way to buy a home.	■ An ARM can be harder to understand than an FRM.
■ If your payment is lower than it would be with an FRM, you can save the extra money for another financial goal.	■ If your payment on the loan is set too low or if there is a payment cap, you could end up owing more money than you did when you closed on the loan (called negative amortization). That happens because your monthly payment doesn't cover all of the interest due, and the unpaid interest gets added to your principal.
	■ Your rate will be adjusted annually. The ARM rate may soon be higher than the FRM you didn't take out.
	■ You can refinance to get into an FRM, but it may be at a *higher* rate and you'll incur refinancing costs.

plain talk

A cap is the limit of how much an interest rate or monthly payment can change based on the terms of the loan.

front, followed by several years of monthly payments, followed by a "balloon" payment that pays the entire remaining loan balance. A balloon mortgage might work if you expect to move, refinance, or receive a big chunk of money from work or family that would cover the balloon payment. Generally, home buyers refinance just before their balloon payment is due. By taking out a traditional mortgage, they are able to make the balloon payment.

Taxes and Your Home

If you buy a home, not only will you get the joy of home ownership, but you may also be able to get the joy of reducing your tax liability by deducting home-ownership related expenses such as points, mortgage loan interest, and real estate taxes. Here are the basic tax-saving elements of home ownership:

Interest—When you pay interest on a qualified home mortgage, you may generally deduct the interest in full as an itemized deduction. The mortgage must be secured by your principal residence or a second residence. For income tax purposes, a principal residence is the one where you live and return to after short absences. You can have only one principal residence at a time. A second residence is one that is for personal purposes only, or, if rented, used for personal purposes for more than the greater of fourteen days or 10 percent of the number of days you rent the home at fair rental value. If you own more than two homes, you may claim the interest deduction on only one as a second residence for any given year.

Points—The points you pay are deductible in full in the year paid as an itemized deduction if certain conditions are met. To qualify, the loan has to be for the purchase or improvement of, and be secured by, your principal residence. Charging of points must be an established practice in your area, and the amount of points cannot be excessive. The amount must be computed as a percentage of the stated principal amount of the mortgage. Finally, the amount you paid at or before closing, plus any points the seller paid, must be at least as much as the points charged. If you refinance, any points paid must be deducted over the life of the loan.

Real Estate Taxes—If you itemize, you can deduct state, local, and foreign real estate taxes you paid on your home, vacation dwelling, or other real property.

Home Equity Credit Lines—Because the debt is secured by your home, interest on the loan is deductible, subject to certain limitations. You may be able to trade nondeductible debt (such as a large credit card balance or vehicle loan) for debt that is deductible. Even though a home equity loan provides tax advantages not available from other loans, never take out a home equity loan unless you are certain you can make the payments. If you fail to repay the loan, one of your most valuable possessions, your home, may be at risk.

See your tax professional for assistance with the tax consequences of buying and owning a home.

Cutting Your Monthly Payments

If you want to pay less per month, there are some ways to do it, but it's going to cost you, either now or later. But if you're living on a tight budget when you buy your home, you may have no choice but to keep your monthly payment to a minimum. Here are some ways to do that:

Pay More Up Front—If you make a bigger down payment, you'll owe less each month. That assumes, of course, that you actually have or can borrow more money to pay up front, which may not be the case if money is tight.

Extend the Loan—Instead of taking out a 15-year loan, consider opting for a 20- or 30-year loan. The interest rate may be slightly higher, and you'll increase the amount of time it takes to pay off the loan, but it will lower your monthly payment.

smart step

Keep track of your mortgage balance. After you've made mortgage payments long enough to build up 20 percent equity in your home, you may be able to cancel the PMI.

117

Paying it off Faster

Just because you sign a 30-year mortgage doesn't mean you have to make monthly payments for the next thirty years. There are ways to expedite the process—particularly if your personal financial picture brightens. Here are a few ways to pay off your loan faster, and save thousands of dollars in interest payments in the process.

Switch to a Shorter Term Mortgage   If your income increases, you may be able to afford higher monthly payments. You might think that you would pay twice as much each month for a 15-year mortgage as you would for a 30-year, because you pay it off twice as fast, but the difference is not nearly as great as you might expect. Generally, you can get a slightly better interest rate on a 15-year mortgage. And, if interest rates should drop after you get your first mortgage, you'll do even better. On a $100,000 mortgage, if your choice is between a 15-year at 7 percent and a 30-year at 7.25 percent, you would pay about $900 a month on the 15-year and about $680 a month on the 30-year. Over the course of the mortgage, you would make total mortgage payments of about $245,000 on the 30-year (including $145,000 in interest), and $162,000 on the 15-year (including $62,000 in interest). That's a savings of $83,000 on a $100,000 mortgage. That's why so many home buyers are willing to pay the extra $200 to $300 a month to fund a 15-year mortgage.

Add a Lump Sum—If you get a bonus, an inheritance, or simply save a large amount of money, you might consider using it to pay down some of the principal on your loan. That can shorten the terms dramatically. For instance, on a 15-year, 6 percent, $100,000 mortgage, if you pay an additional $20,000 after five years, you could cut the mortgage down to about twelve years. Make sure that your loan does not contain any **prepayment penalties**, which are fees some lenders charge for paying a loan before it is due.

plain talk

A prepayment penalty is a fee that is charged to a borrower who pays a loan before it is due. This penalty is not allowed on certain types of loans such as VA or FHA loans.

Make Extra Principal Payments—If you make additional monthly payments, you will experience a decrease in both the mortgage term and the total interest. For instance, if you are scheduled to pay $900 a month on a $100,000, 15-year, 7 percent mortgage, add another $200 if possible for a $1,100 monthly payment. That extra $200 a month will pay off the loan about four years faster. Again, check the terms of your loan for any prepayment penalties that may apply.

Refinance—If interest rates drop enough, you might be able to get a new mortgage with better rates. You may have to pay extra points to refinance, but a better interest rate will generally make it worthwhile in the long run—if you stay in the home for several more years. For instance, if you're paying off a $100,000 loan at 8 percent for fifteen years, you would have to pay about $955 a month (plus taxes). If you could refinance at 6 percent, you would be able to pay the loan off about two and a half years sooner with the same monthly payment.

Using the Equity in Your Home

The best reason to apply for a new mortgage is if interest rates have dropped far enough that you can realize significant savings. But there are other good ways to use the equity in your home. What else can you do with your home equity?

- **Consolidate your consumer debts and roll them into your mortgage.** You can eliminate your consumer debt, lower your total monthly payments, and often get a tax deduction on all your interest because the mortgage is secured by your home. The main problem with this strategy is that if you don't change your spending habits, you could end up in worse shape and put your home in

fast fact

If you've been deducting points over the life of a mortgage and you refinance that mortgage, you can deduct any points not previously deducted in the year of refinancing.

THE CHALLENGE

Ann had been watching as interest rates dropped steadily. She knew refinancing her home would save her money each month. But when she started talking to lenders, she was stunned. She had had some credit problems several years ago after starting a business that failed, and those blemishes were still on her record. Her application for a new loan was rejected by not one, not two, but three separate lenders. She was in a classic dilemma: To improve her financial situation, she needed to cut her expenses, but she couldn't cut her expenses because of her financial problems.

THE PLAN

Ann tried one more time to explain her situation to another lender. The loan specialist suggested a plan of action that could help Ann. The first step was to get a current appraisal for Ann's home. The new appraisal showed that her home had gone up in value. Ann was now able to qualify for a new mortgage that would allow her to drop the expensive private mortgage insurance she had been paying for and use some of the equity in her home to pay off an outstanding loan she had from her failed business.

Her monthly expenses were reduced dramatically. Because interest rates were lower, her monthly payments on the new mortgage also were lower, even though the mortgage itself was a bit more. Ann used some of the monthly difference to pay off her remaining consumer debt. That cut her monthly expenses even more. And when tax time came, she was able to deduct the interest she was paying on the new mortgage.

jeopardy. It may make more sense to simply stop running up more consumer debt.

- **Switch from an adjustable-rate mortgage to a fixed-rate mortgage.** Locking in a fixed rate can help protect you from possible future interest rate increases.
- **Cancel private mortgage insurance when you've built up enough equity and are no longer required to pay that extra money.** The lender will not automatically stop charging you for mortgage insurance—you need to act on it yourself. The savings are well worth the effort.
- **Help pay for college tuition, home improvements, a car, a boat, a vacation home, or some other major purchase.** Or it could help you finance a new business. If you need money, your home could help you get it.

Home Equity Loan or Line of Credit—You don't always have to get a new mortgage to use the equity in your home to generate cash.

- **Home equity loan.** You can get a home equity loan, using your home as collateral. The interest you pay is usually tax-deductible, and it may be much cheaper to get a home equity loan than a new mortgage. Although the interest rate will be higher on the home equity loan, lenders may not charge some of the fees on home equity loans that they do on new mortgages.
- **Home equity line of credit.** This allows you to borrow against home equity as needed using a checkbook or credit card. With a line of credit, you borrow only what you need when you need it, and you pay it back according to the terms of your line of credit. Once you've repaid the loan, you can use the line of credit again for something else, and keep tapping into it as long as you have the line of credit—with no closing costs and no new application procedure. The danger is that a line of credit can lead some consumers into overspending, just like credit cards.

smart step

Paying extra principal can reduce your total interest payments and pay off your home faster. But if you have credit card debt, concentrate on paying that off first.

If you apply for
a reverse mort-
gage, be sure
it's insured so
that the lender
can't foreclose
on the loan
early.

Reverse Mortgage—If you've paid off all or most of your mortgage, you may be able to use a "reverse mortgage" to generate monthly income from your home equity. Instead of paying the lender, the lender pays you. Typically, a reverse mortgage will pay you either a lump sum, fixed monthly payments, a line of credit, or combination of these.

The loan becomes due when the home is no longer your principal residence if you sell the home, move out permanently, or die. The home doesn't have to be sold to pay off the loan, but if it is, any proceeds in excess of the amount owed on the reverse mortgage would go to you or your estate.

Fortunately, reverse mortgage payments aren't taxed, and they won't reduce Social Security and Medicare benefits. The most popular reverse mortgage programs are sponsored by Fannie Mae and require the homeowner to be at least sixty-two years old. There are three primary programs:

- **Home Keeper.** The basic program, Home Keeper, allows you to borrow against the equity in your home. A lender that participates in the program pays you equal monthly payments which continue until the loan is due, allows you to tap a line of credit, or a combination of both. You repay the loan when you sell the home or no longer use it as your principal residence, or your estate pays it when you die. Repayment of the loan will include interest and other financing costs.
- **Home Keeper for Home Purchase.** You can buy a new home with a reverse mortgage loan. You make a down payment as you would normally, but don't have monthly payments. You take out a reverse mortgage for the balance and the home acts as security for the reverse mortgage, which you or your estate repays when you sell or otherwise permanently leave the home.
- **Home Equity Conversion Mortgage.** This is similar to a Home Keeper mortgage, but with two additional payment options. In addition to monthly payments for as long as you occupy the home as a principal residence, line of

credit, or combination of the two, additional payment options also include monthly payments for a specified term or monthly payments for a term combined with a line of credit.

Home ownership has long been considered a part of the American dream. Owning a home can be a smart investment and one that comes with many tax-saving opportunities. Like any investment, a home's value can rise and fall; however, over time, home ownership has been an excellent investment for many people.

the ESSENTIALS

1 Owning a home can help you financially as well as put a roof over your head. Think about how long you expect to stay in one place, whether you can afford a home and maintain it, and what other needs you have for the money.

2 In deciding whether to approve you for a mortgage, lenders will be concerned about what percentage of your overall income your housing costs represent and how well you have met your obligations in the past.

3 Don't give up hope just because you don't have much money for a down payment. The sooner you start saving, the sooner you'll be able to afford a down payment.

4 Your down payment may depend on the price of the home, what interest rate you're willing to accept, and the type of loan you get.

5 Because the interest on home mortgages is generally tax-deductible, explore whether it makes sense for you to use a home equity loan to pay off consumer debt or cover other major financial needs.

8 [SURVIVING THE FEAR FACTOR: Investing Basics for Dealing with Risk]

"There are no secrets to success. It is the result of preparation, hard work, learning from failure."

—Colin Powell

smart step

Sit down with your financial advisor and determine where you are today, where you want to go, and then determine the best route to get you there.

Are you a saver or an investor? You may have wondered what the difference is between saving and investing. Both make your money grow, but the return you earn from accounts that you set up at your bank may be barely enough to keep up with inflation. For the intermediate and long-term goals you identified in Chapter 1, you'll probably need to move beyond the bank and put at least some of your money into other investments. You won't make as much progress toward financing your child's education or your retirement by simply leaving your money in the bank.

Stocks, bonds, and mutual funds have been popular investments for individuals for many years. They offer a simple, effective way to participate in the growth of corporate America and the global economy. And, despite their volatility (fluctuation in value), all three types of investments have proven to be profitable over the long term.

Setting up your investment portfolio can seem like a challenging task if you have never invested. But with a little effort and initiative—either on your own or with a financial advisor and your tax professional—you can join the millions of Americans who are building their investment portfolios. You work hard for your money. Make it work for you. If you can take some time now to learn about investing and start an investment program, your efforts may be rewarded many times over in the years ahead.

Dealing with Risk

Playing it safe by leaving your money in the bank may help you sleep better for now, but not forever. One day, you'll wake up and realize that your money isn't growing fast enough. The years are ticking by, and you may never have enough time to reach your financial goals if you don't get more than a 1 to 3 percent return on your savings.

But why wait to learn that lesson? It's better to take action now. A real risk is not in investing, but rather in *not* investing. If your money doesn't grow at a reasonable rate, you may reach your retirement years without adequate resources.

Types of risks

When evaluating various types of investments, there are many types of risk to consider. The more you know about risk, the better able you'll be to determine your **risk tolerance** as it applies to various investments. You'll also learn ways to manage risk. Here are some risks you'll want to consider:

Market Risk—The risk that an equity investment's value will decline due to the market, as a whole going down

Industry Risk (sector)—The risk of all equities in a particular industry doing poorly

Individual Security Risk—The risk of one particular security's value declining

Economic Risk—The risk of a poor economy affecting the value of investments

Inflation Risk—The risk of inflation eating away at real returns (your return after the effects of taxes and inflation)

Currency Risk—The risk of exchange rates fluctuating (can affect investments in international investments)

Credit Risk—The risk due to the possibility of a particular issue (bond) defaulting or being downgraded

Interest Rate Risk—The risk associated with changing interest rates (rates up equals bond prices down)

plain talk

Risk tolerance is a combination of your attitude toward taking financial risks and your ability to withstand losses.

How Does Risk Affect an Investment?

Risk and reward tend to go hand in hand. The riskier an investment, the more the company must offer to attract investors. For example, a new company with unproven prospects would have to pay a higher interest rate to borrow money than an established company with a solid balance sheet. The lender (that's you when you buy a corporate bond) has to be rewarded for the risk involved. The stock of a young company with low earnings and an uncertain future may be riskier than a blue-chip company with a long history of growth. If the young company doesn't succeed, you, the stockholder, would lose most, if not all, of your investment. If the company begins to turn a consistent profit, its stock could enjoy much greater gains than that of a well-established, blue-chip stock.

Taking investment risks is not the frightening proposition you might think it is—particularly if you have two things on your side:

- **Diversification can cut your risks dramatically.** If you invest in a broad portfolio of stocks, bonds, and mutual funds (and perhaps real estate directly or through a real estate investment trust), you'll give yourself a much better chance of long-term investment success.
- **Time can cut your risks dramatically.** Investments such as individual stocks tend to be volatile in the short term, but over the long term they have typically delivered good returns.

Lower-yielding investments, such as bonds and CDs, will provide a steadier return than stocks. But if you're a long-term investor, short-term results should not be your priority.

Basic Investment Types

Before we look at the relative riskiness of various investments and who should consider various types of investments, you need to understand what the investments are. Here are brief descriptions of some different types of investments:

INVESTMENT	DESCRIPTION
Bank savings accounts	Accounts such as passbook or statement savings accounts. Generally, these accounts pay a low rate of interest.
Certificates of deposit	A short- or long-term interest-bearing savings vehicle. The investor agrees to tie up his or her money for a stated period of time.
Money market accounts	A savings account that pays a competitive rate of interest based on the market for short-term securities. Generally requires a higher balance.
Treasury bills	A short-term federal government security with maturities of three to twelve months. You are loaning money to the U.S. government for a short period of time.
Money market funds	A mutual fund that invests in short-term securities, such as Treasury bills, certificates of deposit, and commercial paper. The share price is kept stable at $1, and dividends are paid at competitive rates. Many money market funds offer limited check writing.
Bonds	A loan to a corporation or government agency. The bond issuer promises to repay you the principal on a specified date (known as the maturity date). For bonds with stated interest, the issuer agrees to pay you interest for the use of your money during the period of the loan.
Annuities	An agreement between you and an insurance company where you pay the insurer a specified amount and, in return, receive regular payments either for life or for a stated period of time. The money grows on a tax-deferred basis until you receive it. There are two basic types of annuities: fixed and variable. If you choose a fixed annuity, the premiums you pay will be invested in fixed-rate instruments such as bonds or mortgages. Fixed annuities have a guaranteed return but do not offer inflation protection. In a variable annuity, your premiums could be invested in a variety of items, ranging from individual stocks and mutual funds to real estate and certificates of deposit. Your return will vary depending on the success of the portfolio.
Mutual funds	An investment vehicle that allows you to pool your money with other investors. A professional money manager then invests the pool of money in a portfolio of securities according to the stated objective of the mutual fund.
Stocks	A share of stock represents your ownership (or equity) position in the company. Your return is based on appreciation of the stock's value and dividends, if any.

smart step

Carefully weigh the trade-off between risk and return. If you find yourself constantly worried about the volitility of your investment portfolio, you may need to consider a less aggressive investment strategy.

The investments described on the preceeding page are listed from least risky to most risky, and savings accounts are included to give you the full picture. The riskiest types of investments (futures and options) are not included because they're generally not practical choices for most investors.

Short-Term Investments

Short-term investments are typically generated from loans by financial institutions for periods of just a few weeks or months. The buying and selling of those loans is known as the "money market," because those short-term loans are considered to be the closest thing to actual cash. Their brief time frame makes short-term investments a safer type of investment.

Because the principal generally remains stable—in some cases, it's even guaranteed—money market funds are often used to protect money that will be invested or spent elsewhere later. If you have a pending need for a specific amount of money—college tuition due next year, a down payment for a home in a year or two—a short-term investment in a money market fund or short-term CD is probably the wisest way to go.

However, don't expect a big return. Your interest rate is likely to be little more than the rate of inflation. In recent years, banks have paid only about 1 to 2 percent on short-term investments. So you'll get only minimal growth on that money—but plenty of safety. Even though short-term investments should generally not be a major part of your long-term investing plan, most portfolios do include at least some of these investments.

The Stock Market

Stocks give you an opportunity to participate in the growth of corporate America. By buying stock, you become a part owner of a business. You can own shares in some of the great companies in America, and you can invest in exciting, up-and-coming small businesses in the hope that they will continue to grow.

Stocks give investors two ways to gain—**capital appreciation** and **dividends**. Not all companies pay dividends. However, many large, well-established companies do pay dividends each quarter. Those dividends—which generally range from about 1 to 5 percent of the stock price per year—come from the company's profits. Many companies raise their dividend each year, giving shareholders an increasing flow of income.

You can also profit from the stock's appreciation. As the company grows and becomes more profitable, its stock tends to increase in value. That's why it's important to both look for companies with growing earnings and diversify by building a portfolio of several stocks from several different industries.

Stocks are best suited for money you won't need for several years. That way, when the market dips as part of its long-term cycle, you'll have some time for the market to rebound before you need the money.

Investing in Bonds

Generally speaking, bonds are considered safer and more conservative than stocks. But while the risks are lower, so is the potential for gain. And the safer the bond, the lower the return. Many investors include both stocks and bonds in their portfolios to provide diversification.

Corporations and government entities issue bonds to raise money. The federal government is the largest issuer of bonds, but many state, local governments, and school districts also issue bonds, as do most major corporations.

Investors are attracted to bonds because of their low risk and steady stream of income. While bond values may fluctuate over the life of the bond, when a bond matures, the holder is paid exactly the amount as stated in the bond agreement. Retired people often use the interest income from their bonds to cover their daily living expenses. However, bonds are not particularly popular for investors who still have a long way to go to build up their retirement accounts. Stocks provide better potential for long-term growth, while bonds offer safety and a steady income. By owning both stocks and bonds, investors can help to minimize the volatility of returns. Even when stocks are down in value, bonds will help balance the portfolio by providing a steady stream of interest income.

There are several different types of bonds available to investors, including:

Treasury Bonds—Treasury bonds are considered the safest bonds on the market because they are issued and guaranteed by the U.S. government. Because of their safety and virtual guarantee against default, Treasuries are considered the benchmark in the bond world. Treasury bonds are issued in denominations of $1,000, $5,000, $10,000, $100,000, and $1 million. In addition to the safety feature of Treasury bonds, they also provide a tax advantage. All interest you earn is exempt from state and local taxes. With their safety, tax advantages, and steady stream of income, why wouldn't everybody put their money in Treasuries? The big drawback to Treasury bonds is their low return. The yield on Treasuries is among the lowest of all interest-bearing investments; however, they may be attractive to conservative investors.

U.S. Savings Bonds—Savings bonds are a form of Treasury security, and come with the same tax advantages and level of safety—as well as the same low return. However, savings bonds are available in smaller denominations. You can buy them in various denominations ranging from $50 to $10,000. Most savings bonds are issued at half their face value (100 percent for Series I). For instance, when you buy a $100 bond, you pay $50. The bond grows at a pre-set interest rate, and is redeemable any time after the first six months (twelve months for Series I). If the bond reaches its original maturity before you redeem it, it automatically enters one or more extension periods, and continues to earn interest. The bonds stop earning interest when they reach final maturity—that's thirty years for Series EE and I bonds, and twenty years for Series HH bonds.

Municipal Bonds—These bonds, commonly known as "muni bonds," are issued by states, cities, counties, towns, villages, and other local taxing authorities. The big draw for municipal bonds is that the interest they pay is exempt from federal income tax. And in most cases, bondholders who live in the state where the bonds are issued do not pay state or local taxes on the interest, either. That's why municipal bonds are popular with individuals who are in a high tax bracket, although they are subject to the alternative minimum tax. However, like treasuries and savings bonds, muni bonds pay a relatively low interest rate.

Corporate Bonds—Corporations also issue bonds to raise money for expansion and other purposes. But, because corporations cannot offer either the guarantee that the government can or the tax-exempt benefits, they must pay a higher rate of interest. Investors who are willing to accept more risk in return for a larger stream of income from the bond investments prefer corporate bonds. Most bonds pay interest semiannually. Corporate bonds typically offer yields of 2 to 6 percent higher than Treasuries.

Junk Bonds—Also known as high-yield bonds, junk bonds are corporate bonds issued by companies with a very high risk level. Newer, smaller companies that need to raise capital to expand their businesses must issue bonds just like the larger corporations. But investors are less willing to buy bonds of a company

smart step

Tax-deferred or tax-free investments can yield higher returns than taxable investments. Consult with your financial advisor and tax professional to determine what is right for you.

TAX-EXEMPT VS. TAXABLE YIELDS						
TAX BRACKET	10%	15%	27%	30%	35%	38.6%
TAX-EXEMPT YIELD (%)	**TAXABLE YIELD (%)**					
4.0	4.44	4.71	5.48	5.71	6.15	6.51
4.5	5.00	5.29	6.16	6.43	6.92	7.33
5.0	5.56	5.88	6.85	7.14	7.69	8.14
5.5	6.11	6.47	7.53	7.86	8.46	8.96
6.0	6.67	7.06	8.22	8.57	9.23	9.77
6.5	7.22	7.65	8.90	9.29	10.00	10.59
7.0	7.78	8.24	9.59	10.00	10.77	11.40
7.5	8.33	8.82	10.27	10.71	11.54	12.21
8.0	8.89	9.41	10.96	11.43	12.31	13.03
8.5	9.44	10.00	11.64	12.14	13.08	13.84
9.0	10.00	10.59	12.33	12.86	13.85	14.66

How to use this chart: Find the line that shows the rate of interest you can receive on a tax-exempt bond. Then find the column that shows your tax bracket. The percentage shown is the interest rate you would need to receive on a taxable bond to have the same after-federal-tax yield as with the tax-exempt bond.

Example: If you're in the 27 percent bracket and you can earn 6 percent on a tax-exempt bond, you should not purchase a taxable bond unless the rate exceeds 8.22 percent.

Source: H&R Block

that they've never heard of when they can buy bonds from solid, well-established companies. Because of the higher risk, smaller companies must pay a higher yield to attract investors. So, while the risk of default is higher with junk bonds, so is the yield. Junk bonds often pay 2 to 5 percent higher than investment-grade corporate bonds.

Zero Coupon Bonds—Instead of making regular interest payments, zero coupon bonds are issued at a deep discount to face value. They slowly grow to face value until the time they reach maturity. There are no interest payments—just an increase in the value of the bond. The advantage of this type of investment is that you know exactly how much money you will have at a specific future date. Unless the bond is tax-exempt, the periodic growth of the bond (the accrued original issue discount) is taxable.

Mutual Funds

Mutual funds have become a favorite investment for many who want to invest in a variety of stocks and bonds. With a single investment, a mutual fund provides professional management and instant diversification at a low cost. Mutual funds invest in a diverse range of stocks or bonds according to the investment goals of the fund. By buying shares of a mutual fund, you become a shareholder of that broad portfolio and, therefore, share in the gains—and losses—that the mutual fund experiences.

You might find it easier to pick a mutual fund (or several funds) for your investment account. However, even mutual fund investors must do some homework. There are about 8,000 mutual funds on the market. When selecting a mutual fund, look for funds that have been among the leaders in total return over the past ten years, and that have had solid, consistent returns that match or beat the market year in and year out. Learn about the funds' objectives and approach to risk. Invest in the ones that match your risk tolerance and goals, while also considering how investing in the funds will impact the diversification of your overall portfolio.

Although the selection process may be difficult, investing in mutual funds is simple. Most fund families have toll-free numbers you can call to set up an account, and they have Web sites that provide more information about their funds. Once you invest in a fund, you can have the dividends from your fund automatically

smart step

Keep accurate records of all shares purchased with reinvested dividends. Their cost increases the basis in the mutual fund and decreases the gain or increases the loss when you sell your shares.

reinvested in additional shares (or mailed to you). You can also have money automatically deducted from your bank account each month to invest in fund shares. That way, without ever writing a check or worrying about your investment options, you can increase your investment in your favorite funds.

Investors can choose from a wide variety of mutual funds, including:

Growth Stock Funds—Generally, these funds invest in stocks that seek long-term growth first and current income second.

Small Stock Funds—If you want a stake in some exciting young companies, invest in a small stock fund. Don't put all of your money into such funds, but small stocks should generally be a part of a well-diversified portfolio.

International and Foreign Stock Funds—You can invest in stocks from around the world by buying an international fund. As part of a diversified portfolio, you may want to consider having a small percentage of your money invested outside the United States. A foreign stock mutual fund is an easy way to do that.

Sector Funds—You can invest in funds that buy only stocks in a specific industry such as technology. In fact, there are funds that focus on nearly every sector of the economy, including computer funds, communications funds, retail funds, bank and financial services funds, energy funds, automotive funds, and others. You probably wouldn't want to put all of your money into a sector fund, but sector funds can be an important part of a diversified portfolio.

Bond Funds—You can choose between government bond funds (which tend to pay the lowest return), corporate bond funds, and high-yield (or junk) bond funds. Despite their diversification, however, bond funds are not necessarily as safe as individual bonds. If interest rates rise, the value of bonds tends to drop—as does the value of a bond fund. If you own an individual bond, you can hold the bond to maturity and redeem your entire principal, regardless of changes in interest rates.

That's not true with bond funds. Bond fund managers must do a lot of buying and selling of bonds in the fund, and when interest rates go up, the value of their overall portfolio declines, and so does your share price. On the other hand, bond funds offer diversification, which is especially important when investing in junk bonds. Individually, junk bonds are fairly risky, but when dozens of junk bonds are chosen by professionals and pooled into a diversified bond fund, it makes the fund less risky. Even if one bond defaults, the others will continue to offer high-yield returns.

Balanced Funds—You can buy funds that invest in both stocks and bonds, providing broad diversification with a single investment.

A financial advisor can help you choose the investments that are right for you.

smart step

Invest equal amounts over time. Dollar-cost averaging is one way to even out price fluctuations and reduce the average cost of investing, though it doesn't guarantee a profit.

Diversification

Investing in a wide range of investments and investing in different sectors or industries can be a key to a successful long-term investment program. Through diversification, you can manage your risks and help reduce the negative impact that a poorly performing individual investment could have on your portfolio. Different types of investments such as stocks or bonds and different investment sectors such as technology or utilities behave differently under various economic conditions. Having the right diversification or mix of investments in your portfolio is an important consideration when developing your investment plan.

Asset allocation Is the way In which your money is divided among various types of investments— for example, stocks, bonds, and short-term investments.

PERFORMANCE OF DIVERSIFIED ASSETS		
TYPE OF INVESTMENT	AVERAGE ANNUAL RETURN 1926-2002	VALUE OF $1 INVESTED 1926-2002
Large cap stocks	10.2%	$ 1,775.34
Small cap stocks	12.1%	$ 6,816.40
Intermediate-term bonds	5.4%	$ 59.05
Long-term bonds	5.5%	$ 59.70
Corporate bonds	5.9%	$ 82.48
T-bills	3.8%	$ 17.48
Inflation	3.1%	$ 10.12

Source: Stocks, Bonds, Bills and Inflation® 2003 Yearbook, ©2003 Ibbotson Associates, Inc. Based on copyrighted works by Ibbotson and Sinquefield. All rights reserved. Used with permission.

Unfortunately, you can't start with a diversified investment portfolio. Diversification is not a simple one-step process. You have to build it from the ground up, one investment at a time, and that can take several years. The key is to start with something—anything—and build from there. Your goal should be to have a well-rounded portfolio within a reasonable period of time.

You can make money from an investment in two ways. You can sell it for more than you paid for it; in that case, you're earning money through growth in the value of your initial investment (your principal). Or, you can receive regular income from your investment, as you would from a loan that was paid back in regular installments over time.

Different types of investments behave differently under various economic conditions. Through diversification and **asset allocation**, you can manage your risks so that if one of your investments does poorly, the others may pick up the slack and keep your overall portfolio on a steady course.

What Is the Right Asset Allocation for You?

The answer will change over time. Young investors may want to consider having more of their money in stocks and mutual funds with better long-term potential, while older investors may want to consider having more money in bonds and CDs that carry less risk and volatility. But no matter what your age, you need a diversified portfolio that includes a variety of investments.

Even if you're retired, you may need to keep some stocks and stock mutual funds in your portfolio to help you keep your money growing. A person who retires at age sixty-five could still live twenty to thirty more years (and possibly longer). Your investment choices should reflect your need for security and your need for growth.

> No matter your age, diversification should be a vital part of your investment plan.

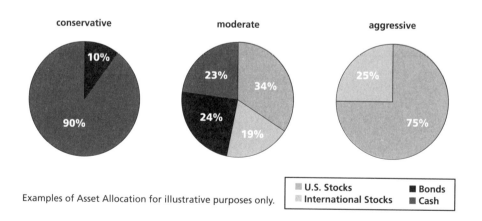

conservative
10%
90%

moderate
23%
34%
24%
19%

aggressive
25%
75%

Examples of Asset Allocation for illustrative purposes only.

U.S. Stocks
International Stocks
Bonds
Cash

THE CHALLENGE

Joyce and Greg, both age fifty-nine, have worked all their lives and now are looking forward to retirement. Joyce has a 401(k) plan where she works and Greg has a defined benefit plan that will pay him a monthly pension for life when he retires. The couple also has some appreciated vacant land they purchased years ago, and some money in a bank savings account.

"We knew our finances would change when we retire, but we didn't have a specific plan in mind," said Greg.

THE PLAN

Joyce and Greg made an appointment with a financial advisor recommended by a friend. The advisor explained that Joyce's 401(k) plan would be distributed to her when she retired. The advisor suggested that Joyce have her employer transfer the entire proceeds from the account directly to an IRA at Joyce's bank or brokerage firm so she could continue deferring paying tax on the money until she withdrew it gradually during retirement. "He further suggested investing most of the money in bonds to provide security and steady income, but to also put a bit of it in stocks so our money would hopefully keep growing," said Joyce.

The advisor further suggested selling the vacant land and investing the proceeds in an annuity. "The advisor pointed out that the land produced no cash income, and, in fact, was costing us money in the form of real estate taxes each year," explained Greg.

On a final note, the advisor suggested that while they were still working, they each invest the maximum allowed in Roth IRAs, even if they had to take money from their bank account to do so. "We learned that contributions to Roth IRAs aren't tax-deductible, but when we take the money out during retirement, all the proceeds, including earnings, are tax-free," said Greg. "We feel much better now knowing that we have a sound financial plan for our retirement," added Joyce.

Creating a Tax-Efficient Investment Plan

The goal of your investment plan is almost certainly to maximize your wealth. Working hand-in-hand with your investment plan, the goal of your investment tax plan should be to help you minimize your tax liability. Regardless of the investments you select for your portfolio, they will all have tax consequences. In order to have a tax-efficient investment plan, you'll need to select the right mix of investments, generally combining both before-tax and after-tax investments to maximize your wealth and minimize your taxes. Once your plan is in place, you'll know when the time is right to take advantage of some of the many tax-saving opportunities that occur throughout the year. Your financial advisor and tax professional can help you to create a plan that is right for your personal situation.

Are Investment-Related Expenses Tax-Deductible?

Many expenses related to investments that product taxable income are tax-deductible. However, any expenses related to tax-exempt investments cannot be deducted.

Here is a short list of deductible investment expenses. These expenses are deductible as miscellaneous itemized deductions if your total miscellaneous itemized deductions exceed 2 percent of your adjusted gross income (AGI).

- **Depreciation on a home computer used for investment activities** (limited and keep a time log)
- **Fees for online trading** (restricted to account maintenance-related fees)
- **Investment club operating expenses** (your share)
- **Investment fees, custodial fees, trust administration fees, and other expenses you paid that are necessary to collect investment income or maintain your taxable investments**
- **IRA fees billed and paid separately from your IRA contribution**

- **Safe-deposit box rental if the box is used to store stocks, bonds, or investment documents**
- **Subscriptions to investment magazines and newsletters**

Remember, fees and commissions for buying and selling an asset are not deductible; instead, they increase your basis and thus reduce your gain or increase your loss when you sell or otherwise dispose of the asset.

You've probably heard of investors who attempt to time the market by purchasing stock when the price is low and selling stock when the stock is high. Timing in tax planning is just as important.

Your Investments and How They Are Taxed

Investment income in the form of interest, dividends, and capital gains is usually (but not always) taxable.

- **Interest.** Most interest from your investments is taxable. Note, however, that most municipal bond interest escapes federal tax and may escape state tax as well. Interest on federal obligations, such as savings bond interest, is taxable on your federal return, but not on your state return.
- **Dividends.** Dividends come in three varieties. Ordinary dividends are taxable. Capital gain distributions are taxable as long-term capital gains. Nontaxable distributions are just that: nontaxable. They represent a return of principal and reduce your basis in the investment.
- **Capital gains and losses.** When you sell investments—such as shares of stock, bonds, shares of a mutual fund, or certain real estate—at a gain, the gain is generally treated as a capital gain. Conversely, when you sell at a loss, a capital loss is generated.

Except for Treasury securities and Government National Mortgage Association (GNMAs), there are no guarantees that any investment will produce either growth or income. Both growth and income have their advantages. In general, investments that focus on growth tend to have higher potential—along with greater risk.

Remember that the most important thing is to make sure you have a sound investment plan to meet your goals. Work with your financial advisor to help choose the investments that are right for you.

smart
step

Start Now!

Calculate
how your
investments
can grow over
time.

Log on to
hrblock.com/advisor

the ESSENTIALS

1 Three key reasons for investing: to get growth from an increase in the value of your initial investment; to get regular payments of income from your investment; and to preserve the dollar value of your initial investment. An ideal portfolio addresses all three needs.

2 To determine how your money should be invested, first determine your priorities and needs. Then determine your time horizon and risk tolerance.

3 Different investments have different types of risk. Generally, the higher the potential return, the higher the level of risk.

4 Remember that an investment's level of risk can be different in the short term than in the long term.

9 [PAYING FOR COLLEGE:]
The Art of Getting Grants,
Loans, and Scholarships

"Education's purpose is to replace an empty mind with
an open one."

—Malcolm Forbes

I f you have a family, you know that sending your children to college may be a daunting financial challenge. College is expensive and the costs continue to rise annually. For students attending private colleges, costs can exceed $100,000 for a four-year degree. Even the public colleges and universities are asking for more money these days. No matter where your children attend college, the costs could definitely tax your budget.

But there are ways to send your children to college without going too far into debt. There are grants, loans, scholarships, work-study programs, and other ways to cut the costs of college. Most parents use a combination of their own money (savings and/or current income) and other items, such as grants, loans, and tax credits, to pay for their children's college educations.

Financial aid formulas assume about 5.6 percent of your assets and income each year can go to pay college tuition. For money held in a child's name, the percentage is much higher—about 35 percent. The good news is that lenders don't consider the money in your retirement account and equity in your home in determining college aid.

Gifts, Grants, Loans, and Scholarships

T here are three major types of financial aid: gift money, which doesn't have to be paid back; loans, some of which are subsidized; and work-study opportunities. Aid packages may change each year—the amount may be reduced or increased, or more money may come from other loans or grants.

Grants—Grants are the gold standard of financial aid. They don't have to be repaid, and you don't have to work for them. Some grants are based on merit, and some are based on financial need. Be sure to apply. Otherwise, you may not be eligible for other student loans.

Pell Grants—Pell grants are the most common federal grants. They are awarded to undergraduate students based on need and family income. Applying for a Pell grant is the first step toward qualifying for any subsidized student loans. The maximum award is about $4,000 per year. For students with even greater needs, the federal government offers supplemental educational opportunity grants that can provide an additional $1,000 to $4,000. When you get an answer to your **Free Application for Federal Student Aid** (FAFSA) request, you will be told whether you qualify for a grant and how much you can get.

Scholarships—Scholarships, like grants, do not have to be repaid. They can be based on financial need, merit, or other factors. In fact, if a college supporter likes a student or a family well enough, he or she could establish a philanthropic scholarship fund for the student.

The college admissions office may automatically consider an applicant for grants and scholarships that it administers or is familiar with, but there's no guarantee. You may have to locate available grants and scholarships on your own. There are scholarship search services available, but many of the low-cost services simply notify you about money for which you're already being considered through your various student aid applications.

Student Loans—The federal government provides low-cost loans for college education. Depending on which program your school participates in, money for such loans is provided by either the federal government or private lenders.

Need-based loans usually carry lower interest rates than other types of loans. A student who qualifies for special subsidized loans won't have to pay any interest until he or she graduates. And unless the student's income after graduation is over a certain amount—$50,000 to $65,000 for singles, $100,000 to $130,000 for married couples—interest on student loans is also tax-deductible. These amounts are for 2003 and are adjusted each year for inflation.

plain talk

FAFSA is short for Free Application for Federal Student Aid. This form is the basis for virtually all financing of educational costs. It is submitted by students and their families in January each year.

smart step

Find out if a school's financial aid package drops after freshman year, and whether that aid shifts from grants to loans. This information will help you compare future costs.

Most need-based loans are made to the students rather than the parents. Interest is paid by the federal government until after the student graduates. There are several types of federal loan programs available, including:

Perkins Loans—These are available for students with exceptional financial needs. Perkins loans, available for both graduate and undergraduate students, have a 5 percent fixed rate. Students can borrow up to $3,000 a year, not to exceed a total of $15,000. Graduate students can borrow up to $5,000 a year and $30,000 total. However, there are limits on the number of students who can qualify at each college.

Stafford Loans—Interest rates for subsidized Stafford loans are a little higher than Perkins loans, but are still offered at a favorable rate. They are offered through private lenders, and participants are given several options for repayment. Undergraduate and graduate students who can demonstrate financial need are eligible. A student who doesn't qualify for a subsidized Stafford loan may still be able to get a low-cost federal Stafford loan. However, because it is not subsidized, the student will owe all the interest on the loan. Payments can sometimes be postponed; the lender will simply add the interest to the amount of the loan and raise the monthly payments due after graduation.

PLUS Loans—Parents who pass a credit check are eligible for a PLUS (Parent Loans for Undergraduate Students) loan. The amount of the loan is typically equal to the cost of attendance minus any financial aid. Parents must begin to repay the loan within sixty days of the final loan disbursement for the academic year. The interest rate varies, but cannot exceed 9 percent.

Many parents may find that they will have to borrow additional money outside the financial aid programs to fund college expenses from such traditional sources as banks, savings and loans, home equity lenders, and 401(k) plans.

FINANCIAL AID TYPES AT A GLANCE			
	GIFT	**LOAN**	**TAX CREDIT**
Need-based	Pell grant Scholarship	Subsidized Stafford	Hope Scholarship Lifetime Learning
Not need-based	Scholarship	Unsubsidized Stafford, PLUS (Parent Loans for Undergraduate Students)	Phased out at higher income levels

Help from Your Child

Another form of financial aid is work-study programs that provide work opportunities that pay in tuition credits or provide money that can be used to help pay tuition. Summer jobs also can provide income, though it will be counted at a higher rate than parental income in structuring a financial aid package.

Your child can also help his or her own cause by excelling in high-school academics and participating in extracurricular activities. Colleges want the top-caliber students—those who not only get good grades but also participate in activities such as band, choir, drama, sports, debate, and scholastic teams. If your son or daughter becomes a captain of a sports team, debate team, chess team, or other organization, that can also be a big plus with college admission officers.

Qualifying for Financial Aid

Shopping for the perfect college for your son or daughter is no easy job, but it may seem like child's play compared with the mountain of forms you'll have to fill out to learn if you qualify for financial aid. But it is well worth the effort. Free money is hard to come by, but the government and other entities

smart step

To compare student aid from more than one college, look beyond the bottom line. Check to see how much of the aid package must be repaid, and what interest will cost you.

pass out millions of dollars a year for college assistance. Almost three-quarters of all college students qualify for some type of aid. Even if you're not sure you'll qualify, go through the process anyway. You may be pleasantly surprised.

Applying for Financial Aid

Here is a step-by-step checklist for the process:

- [ ] **After researching colleges, apply to a few favorites.** Choose carefully, because most colleges charge an application fee and those can add up quickly.
- [ ] **In the fall of the year before your child goes to college, check to see what type of state, campus-based, and private financial assistance might be available.** Application deadlines for these special grants are usually earlier than the deadlines for federal financial aid forms.
- [ ] **After December 31, fill out a Free Application for Federal Student Aid (FAFSA).** You can't apply before January 1, but submit the application soon after December 31.
- [ ] **After you've submitted your FAFSA, you will receive a Student Aid Report (SAR) that will tell you if you qualify for a Pell grant.** It will also show you how much to expect to pay toward college costs from your own pocket, that's your Estimated Family Contribution (EFC).
- [ ] **Designate on your FAFSA to which colleges you'd like your SAR sent.** Each institution uses its own formula to determine how much it will cost the student to go to college (including room, board, and books). The college then subtracts the EFC and decides how much of the difference it is willing to make up in grants, scholarships, loans, and work-study opportunities. The college's decision will depend to a great degree on how badly the college wants your child.
- [ ] **Compare the total financial-aid package offered by each college you're considering.** If it's not enough, you have other options.

☐ **Make sure no special circumstances have been overlooked, and that all your financial information is accurate.**

☐ **You may be able to negotiate with a college based on what you're being offered elsewhere.** The more a college wants your child, the more it will typically offer in aid. If your child is an exceptional student or an outstanding musician or athlete, for example, that could help your child's chances.

☐ **Finally, look at non-subsidized tuition sources, such as private loans.**

Special College Savings Plans

I f you have a few years before your children head to college, you might be able to get more for your college savings if you do it through a tax-favored college savings program. There are plenty of options to help you in the years leading up to college and beyond, and all of them have important tax implications. Check out some of these tax-savvy options:

- **529 Qualified Tuition Programs** (i.e., college savings accounts and prepaid tuition plans)
- **Coverdell education savings accounts** (also known as education savings accounts or ESAs)
- **Roth and traditional IRAs**
- **UTMA or UGMA accounts** (custodial accounts)
- **Student loan interest and tuition fees deductions**
- **Hope and lifetime learning credits**
- **Stocks**
- **Series EE or Series I U.S. government savings bonds**

Let's take a look at each of them.

smart step

Start Now!

Estimate how much you'll need to save to fund a college education.

Log on to

hrblock.com/advisor

Distributions
from 529 plans
for qualified
educational
expenses are
free of federal
income tax.

529 Qualified Tuition Programs (QTPs)

A great place to start your child's college fund is through college savings plans, also known as 529 plans. Formerly only states could establish these plans, but now private educational institutions can also sponsor their own plans. Distributions from 529 state-sponsored plans for qualified expenses escape federal income tax and may be free of state income tax as well. Distributions from private institution 529 plans used for qualified expenses will be exempt beginning in 2004. In addition, some states offer a deduction for contributions.

The 529 plans come in two varieties: college savings plans and prepaid tuition plans.

College Savings Plans—For a minimal amount, anyone—parents, relatives, and even friends—can open a college savings plan and contribute regularly to build a tax-free college fund for a child. Your investment grows tax-free for as long as you remain invested in the plan. Plus, if your family's college plans change, you may change the beneficiary of the plan to another family member without federal income tax consequences.

Benefits of the 529 Savings Plan

- **They're a terrific tax break.** Earnings are tax-free, and withdrawals from state-sponsored plans for qualified educational expenses are exempt from federal income taxes.
- **They're easy to set up.** Simply choose an investment option—a large-cap fund, a balanced fund, or a bond fund, for example—and contribute to the fund regularly.
- **Many are deductible on your state tax return.** Some states allow you to deduct your contributions on your state return. Because rules vary from state to state, be sure to check with your state tax office for details.

- **You will likely get professional help.** Some of the best-known money managers in the United States offer state 529 college savings plans. Once you sign up and begin contributing, the plan manager will take care of the rest, including management and administration of the fund. As with any investment, check on the plan's past performance before you invest.
- **How the money is withdrawn is up to you.** If your child decides not to go to college, you can transfer the fund to another beneficiary. If the money is not used for qualified educational expenses, the earnings are taxable and may be subject to a 10 percent penalty.
- **They're flexible.** In most cases, 529 plans are open to state residents and nonresidents alike. Under the tax laws enacted in 2001, you can now roll your 529 plan over from one state to another with no tax consequence or penalty. This might be a big consideration if you expect to move at any point during when your child is young.
- **They're generous.** Generally, you have the ability to invest more compared to other education-related savings plans.
- **They're good for estate planning.** Contributions to 529 plans are powerful estate planning options for grandparents, because the money is not included in a taxable estate.

Most states do have limits, but many are generously high and some allow in excess of $200,000 to be saved tax-free. So what if you don't happen to live in one of those states? Don't worry, because many states will allow you to participate, regardless of where you live. But check carefully because some states require that the contributor or student be a resident.

Money invested in a 529 college savings plan isn't just for college tuition. You can also use plan money toward room and board, fees, and other expenses. There are no age limits, so even older Americans with a desire to go back to school can participate.

Investigate the past performance of a 529 plan before
investing.

There are some potential downsides to investing in a 529 college savings plan. If your plan has limited investment options, it may be a challenge to get the performance you want or need. Also be aware that eligibility for financial aid may be affected by the account or distributions.

What to Look for in a 529 College Savings Plan

Here is what to search for:

- **A plan with many options.** Check for plans with a wide variety of investment options.
- **Reasonable fees.** Generally, fees should be in line with mutual funds that are similar.
- **Consistent performance.** Double-check the plan's past performance. A plan with lots of ups and downs is something to avoid.

Prepaid Tuition Plans—These plans are known for helping you lock in tomorrow's tuition costs at today's prices. In return for a lump sum, or a series of payments, the state guarantees to cover your child's tuition and fees at a state college or university. Generally speaking, your contributions will be invested by the plan to grow at a rate sufficient to match the anticipated inflation rate of tuition at these state schools. As with college savings accounts, you may also change the beneficiary of the plan to another family member without federal income tax consequences if your child's college plans change.

Drawbacks to prepaid tuition plans include earning a rate of return that only attempts to match the projected rise in tuition costs for the state schools. So if your child gets accepted to Yale, you can use the money you invested in the State U. prepaid college plan to send him or her to school in Connecticut, but it may not cover all the expenses. Also be aware that eligibility for financial aid may be affected by participation in the plan.

Coverdell Education Savings Accounts

The Coverdell education savings account is another college savings plan with strong tax benefits. These accounts are also called ESAs. Once known as "education IRAs," ESAs are similar to 529 plans, except they give you somewhat more freedom in how you can allocate the money saved in the accounts. ESAs don't apply only to college: You can withdraw money tax-free to pay for qualified elementary, secondary, and higher education tuition, fees, and expenses. You can invest in both a 529 plan and an ESA for the same beneficiary in the same year. Now more Americans are using both to meet their education planning needs.

ESAs do have limits. Annual contributions are capped at $2,000 per beneficiary, and you don't receive a tax deduction for your contributions. The real value of the account is the tax-free status of funds when withdrawn for qualified education expenses. If your household's **modified adjusted gross income** (MAGI) exceeds $190,000 ($95,000 on a single return), the allowable contribution will be reduced or eliminated. If you find yourself in this situation, you might want to have a grandparent handle the investment for you. You could give $2,000 to the grandparent, who in turn could make the contribution for you (assuming he or she is eligible).

Contributions to ESAs must generally be made before the beneficiary turns eighteen years old, and the money must generally be distributed before age thirty, along with the plan's earnings. Any unused balance can be rolled over to another child's account. Because many financial institutions offer ESAs, it's relatively easy to switch accounts. In addition, you can claim a Hope credit or lifetime learning credit in the same year that you take tax-free ESA withdrawal. But you cannot use the same expenses claimed for the Hope or the lifetime learning credit and the ESA distribution.

plain talk

Modified adjusted gross income (MAGI) is the sum of your adjusted gross income, plus certain tax-favored items you deducted or excluded.

THE CHALLENGE

José and Christina agreed that they wanted to give their children the best possible start in life, which included a college education. José had been forced to drop out of college to care for his elderly parents. When he returned to finish his degree, he had to work nights and weekends to afford tuition. He and Christina wanted to ensure that their children would not have to do the same. After reading an article about the skyrocketing cost of education, Christina became worried that the education savings account she and her husband had been investing in for their oldest son's education might not cover all of his college expenses.

Christina had been reading about 529 college savings plans and learned that this type of an account could also provide great tax breaks and offer many investment options. Christina decided that she needed to get more information.

THE PLAN

Christina called a financial advisor and scheduled an appointment. The advisor thoroughly explained the benefits of 529 plans and mentioned that Christina and José would control the account. "I'd heard a story about another kind of account in which the money was wasted on expensive electronic gear and parties," said Christina. "I don't think my son would do that, but I needed to be sure."

Christina's financial advisor showed her the variety of investment options for 529 plans, and explained how the funds could be shifted periodically to gain higher returns or minimize the risks to the account balance as her son gets closer to college age. Christina left the appointment confident that a 529 plan would help her and José get the funding for their son's college education back on schedule. "I'm going to start investing today for my son's future," added Christina.

Roth and Traditional IRAs

Both Roth and traditional IRAs have proven to be practical investment tools. Not only do they provide excellent retirement savings benefits, but both can be used for college savings, too. You can take distributions from your Roth or traditional IRA for qualified higher education expenses without paying the 10 percent additional tax that is levied on early (under age fifty-nine and a half) distributions. While you won't have to pay the early distribution penalty, the amount of the distribution included in your income is computed in the usual manner. Also be aware that these accounts and withdrawals could affect the ability to get financial aid. See Chapter 10 for more on IRAs.

UTMA or UGMA Accounts

UTMA and UGMA are acronyms for the Uniform Transfers/Gifts to Minors Act. These custodial accounts are losing popularity as other education savings vehicles have been introduced. In the past, these accounts were very popular and played an important role in many families' college savings programs. One advantage to using a custodial account to save for college is its ability to reduce the family's tax bill. Until age fourteen, the first $750 of a child's investment earnings is tax-free, and the next $750 is taxed at the child's rate (usually 10 percent). After that, the parents' marginal rate applies.

There are some advantages to UTMA and UGMA accounts, but the benefits derived from other plans (529 plans and ESAs) significantly diminish the attractiveness of this approach to college savings. Another important point about custodial accounts is that your contributions to the account are considered an irrevocable gift. Once the student reaches the age of majority (usually eighteen or twenty-one), the account belongs to the student, and he or she can use the money for anything—like a shiny, new Corvette for an all-expenses-paid road

fast fact

With a Coverdell ESA, you can withdraw money tax-free to pay for qualified elementary, secondary, and higher education tuition, fees, and expenses.

smart step

If you're planning to take out a student loan, use the loan proceeds *exclusively* for qualified higher education costs. Interest on mixed-use loans doesn't qualify for the student loan interest deduction.

trip. Also be aware that ownership of a custodial account may cause the student to qualify for less financial aid.

If you've invested in a UTMA or UGMA account and want to invest the assets in a 529 plan, you must sell the securities, report any gains on the child's return, and put the cash into the 529 plan. Finally, another note of caution: Unlike a 529 plan, you won't be able to change the beneficiary of the custodial account and name another child as the beneficiary.

Student Loan Interest Deduction

If you obtained a student loan to help pay for college expenses, you can deduct up to $2,500 annually of the interest you pay on the loan. You can take this write-off whether or not you itemize deductions. This deduction applies to interest on almost any loan (not just federal student loans) that you used exclusively for qualified higher education expenses for yourself, your spouse, or for a person who was your dependent at the time you borrowed the money.

Before 2002, the deduction for student loan interest was available only for the first sixty months that interest payments were due. For 2002 and later years, the sixty-month limit no longer applies. If you stopped taking this deduction because your sixty-month time limit expired, start taking it again.

The following chart discusses some of the differences among the various options for funding college expenses. Generally, you may not claim more than one benefit for the same education expense. Check with your tax professional to determine which option is best for you.

COMPARISON OF TAX BENEFITS FOR EDUCATION

	Savings Bond Interest Exclusion	529 Qualified Tuition Programs*	Coverdell ESA*	Traditional and Roth IRAs	Student Loan Interest Deduction	Tuition and Fees Deduction	Lifetime Learning Credit	Hope Credit
What is the benefit?	Interest is not taxed	Earnings are not taxed		No 10% additional tax on early distributions	Deduct the interest even if you don't itemize	Deduct expenses even if you don't itemize	Credits reduce your tax dollar-for-dollar	
What is the annual limit?	Amount of interest used for qualifying expenses	None	$2,000 contribution per beneficiary	Amount of qualifying expenses	$2,500	Up to $3,000 per family	Up to $1,000 per family	Up to $1,500 per student
What education applies?	All undergraduate and graduate study		Elementary, secondary, undergraduate, and graduate study	All undergraduate and graduate study				1st and 2nd years of undergraduate study
Are benefits limited by income?	Yes	No	Yes	No	Yes	Yes	Yes	Yes
What are some of the other conditions that apply?**	Applies only to qualified Series EE bonds issued after 1989 and Series I bonds	Distributions of earnings not used for qualified higher education expenses are subject to an additional 10% tax	Most beneficiaries must use up accounts or transfer them to a qualified relative before age 30	Taxable income from the distribution is computed using the usual rules	Loan proceeds must have been used exclusively for qualified educational expenses	Cannot claim both this deduction and a tax credit for education expenses for the same student in one year. Qualified expenses must be reduced by a tax-free distribution from a Coverdell ESA, QTP, and by excluded interest from savings bonds used for education		Can be claimed only for 2 years. Must be enrolled at least half-time in a degree program. No history of a felony drug conviction

* Any nontaxable withdrawal is limited to the amount that does not exceed qualifying educational expenses.
** Other conditions may apply. Please consult your tax professional or IRS Publication 970 for more details.

Source: H&R Block

The Hope Credit

The Hope credit allows you a tax credit of up to $1,500 for each qualifying full-time student who meets the following four qualifications. He or she must:

1. Be in his or her first two years of post-secondary education
2. Be enrolled in a program that leads to a degree or other recognized educational credential
3. Be enrolled at least half-time for at least one academic period during the year
4. Have no history of a felony drug conviction

Under the Hope credit, you can claim 100 percent of the first $1,000 and 50 percent of the next $1,000 of qualified expenses, which include tuition, fees, and books that must be purchased from the educational institution. This is a per-child credit, meaning you'll receive a tax credit of up to $1,500 for each qualifying student dependent you claim. As with the other tax credits, your MAGI affects your benefits. The Hope credit begins phasing out when your MAGI exceeds certain limits, which are adjusted annually for inflation. For more information see IRS Publication 970.

The Lifetime Learning Credit

Requirements for the lifetime learning credit are less restrictive than for the Hope credit, but the lifetime learning credit provides less generous benefits. This credit is available for expenses relating to all years of post-secondary education, including graduate-level courses. In addition, there is no pursuit-of-a-degree or at-least–half-time enrollment requirement, and the felony drug conviction rule does not apply.

For 2003, the credit is equal to 20 percent of the first $10,000 you pay for qualified expenses for all eligible students in your family. Thus, the maximum credit you can claim for your family is limited to $2,000 annually. Your MAGI can affect the amount of your credit in the same manner as the Hope credit.

The best time to start planning for college is, of course, as soon as possible after your child or grandchild is born. As with other investments, you need to start saving while time is still on your side. There are plenty of options to help you in the years leading up to college and beyond, and all of them have important tax implications. Your tax professional or financial advisor can be a valuable resource in that regard.

fast fact

the ESSENTIALS

1 College costs continue to rise annually, so get an early start saving for your child's college education. The earlier you start, the more help you'll get from compounded earnings.

2 Fill out the FAFSA form and submit it as soon as possible after January 1 of the year your child will start college—even if you don't think you qualify for financial aid.

3 State-sponsored college savings plans and prepaid tuition plans, also known as 529 plans, are great tax savers. Distributions from state-sponsored 529 plans for qualified expenses are free from federal income tax and often state income tax as well. Some states even allow a deduction for contributions to these plans.

4 Coverdell education savings accounts have many of the same advantages of 529 plans, but they allow you a wider choice of investments. You can withdraw money from an ESA tax-free to pay for qualified elementary, secondary, and higher education expenses.

5 The tax code provides additional opportunities to help you fund college education expenses. Consult with your tax professional about deductions such as for tuition and fees and credits such as the Hope and Lifetime learning credits.

The Hope and lifetime learning credits are nonrefundable. Any credit remaining after your tax liability has been reduced to zero will not be refunded to you.

10 [PLANNING YOUR RETIREMENT: Where Will the Money Come From?]

"If I had known I was going to live this long I would
have taken better care of myself."
—Eubie Blake

Before you take a retirement distribution from an employer plan, talk to a tax professional about the available options.

Many Americans reach their retirement years financially unprepared. As a result, they are forced to either continue working or live on a shoe-string, skimping on everything from trips and entertainment to food and clothes. Your senior years can be your golden years, but they could be difficult if you're having to watch every penny. You'll thank yourself later if you can maintain a consistent retirement savings program while you're working.

That's become more difficult in recent years, with more individuals working for themselves and more businesses cutting back on contributions to their employees' retirement plans. Many companies have dropped traditional pension plans that are paid for and managed by the company, and have replaced them with do-it-yourself retirement plans such as 401(k) plans.

On the bright side, the government has done its best to offer workers incentives to save for retirement. With tax-favored IRAs and employment-based retirement plans such as 401(k) plans, you can save on income taxes now and shelter earnings from taxes as the money in the account grows. The best approach, whether you work for yourself or a company that has an employee-contribution retirement plan, is to have the money automatically deducted from your paycheck or bank account every month. That way, it's locked up before you ever have a chance to spend it. You're paying yourself first.

Retirement Myths

How can so many people make it through forty to fifty years of hard work, day in and day out, and still have nothing left for retirement? If you work from age twenty to age sixty-five, forty-five years in all, it would seem reasonable that at some point you could put money away for retirement. Here are some of the leading retirement misconceptions. If you recognize yourself, maybe you can adjust your approach to retirement savings in time.

Myth: I can always work longer if I have to.

Reality: Maybe—but what if your health doesn't permit it? That's one reason most people retire at age sixty-five. Their energy levels decline, health problems increase, and working every day becomes increasingly difficult. If you prepare financially for retirement, you can give yourself a choice. If you want to keep working, great, but if you can't work, or you don't have the energy or desire to keep working, then a solid retirement savings plan will give you the option of walking away from the work force, or cutting back to a much lighter load.

Myth: I'm really going to get serious about saving for retirement—someday.

Reality: This is a common excuse, and it's understandable. First you have to save for a home, then you have children, which seems to take every penny you can bring home, and then you have to pay for college for the kids. Once that's over, you're nearly ready for retirement. So somehow, in the midst of all those other financial obligations, you need to figure out how to put some money away for your retirement. And you need to figure that out now—not someday.

Myth: It's too late for me.

Reality: Time only goes one way. You probably have more options than you think, but the longer you wait to figure it out, the more financially strapped you'll be when retirement arrives. Even if you're in your fifties or early sixties, cut back on your spending, and save. You'll be grateful later for every dollar you save now.

smart step

To provide the beneficiaries of your IRAs and employer plans the most choices for how to receive the IRA or plan assets, be sure they are named as beneficiaries on the IRA or plan document, not only in your will.

Myth: I don't have any money left over to save.

Reality: Having money deducted automatically from your paycheck can help you save without giving it a thought. Save first, spend what's left over. If there isn't enough left over to meet your expenses, figure out what expenses you can cut or how you can increase your income. If there is nothing left to cut and you're still living from paycheck to paycheck, then maybe consider some other career options.

Myth: I've got more important things to worry about.

Reality: That's what you think now. When you're seventy and you're having problems paying the heating bill, these present-day priorities may seem a little less important.

Myth: I'll get by on my Social Security.

Reality: Social Security is a supplement—it's not a livable wage. Some financial professionals view it as one of the three legs of the retirement stool. The other legs are your retirement plans and your personal savings and investments. Other advisors recommend that their clients not count on Social Security at all.

The Hurdle

A sense of hopelessness sometimes keeps people from ever getting serious about a retirement savings program. They feel they're so far behind that they will never have enough money to retire. However, most people underestimate their true worth. That financial hurdle may not be nearly as high as you think. Once you recognize how much you're already worth, you may be motivated to save more. Financial experts say you'll need 70 to 80

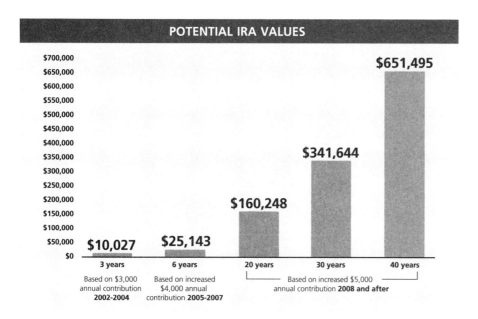

This chart assumes maximum IRA contributions beginning on January 1, 2002 with an annual compounded interest rate of 5.5%. Calculation assumes that the increased contribution limit will be extended beyond 2010. Your rate may vary.

percent of your pre-retirement income after you retire, although you may be able to get by on considerably less. Here are some factors that may make retirement a little easier.

Own Your Home—If you're currently in the process of buying your own home, by the time you retire, it may be completely paid for. That means that one of your biggest financial burdens—that monthly home payment—will be lifted from your shoulders, making your monthly budget that much more tolerable.

Move to a Smaller Home—Once you're retired and the children are gone, you may not need as big a home. You can move to a smaller home (or condominium). And because you won't have to make that daily commute, you'll have a lot more flexibility in where you move, so you can probably get a nice home at a good price. The difference in price between the home you sell and the home you buy could be substantial enough to put tens of thousands of dollars into your pocket.

Children Gone—With no children at home—or in college—you won't face the same expenses in retirement that you face while you're raising a family.

Lower Expenses—Your home payments and childrens' costs won't be the only thing missing from your monthly budget. Once you retire, you may not have to spend as much for clothing and dry cleaning, commuting to work, eating lunches out, and other work-related expenses. However, the typical financial advice that you'll need only 70 to 80 percent of your pre-retirement income can be misleading if you plan to travel and participate in activities that can cost more than your previous work-related expenses.

Inheritance—Do you have any close relatives who may leave you something in their wills? Your parents' retirement nest egg might become part of your own retirement nest egg (or yours and your siblings'). However, don't count your chickens before they hatch.

Social Security—It won't pay all the bills, but it will pay a few of them. The more you can add to this retirement supplement, the better off you'll be. The maximum annual benefit for a person who retired in 2003 at age sixty-five was $20,892. To qualify for Social Security, you need to work for at least ten years. The more years you work and contribute, the more you'll receive from Social Security.

A Side Job—Once you retire, you may not ever want a full-time job again, but you might enjoy working part-time or as a consultant for a few more years. That will keep you active and in touch with the outside world, while bringing in some money to supplement your other income sources. In fact, if you start a small income-producing business in your spare time, maybe by the time you retire, it will be a going concern. You can rely on the income from that business (or a part-time job) to help provide for a prosperous and fulfilling retirement.

Pension—If you're lucky enough to have a pension coming from your place of employment, it, combined with Social Security, could certainly help you get through retirement. However, many businesses have cut back on retirement plans or expect employees to contribute most of the funds from their own pay-checks.

Tax-Wise Saving for Retirement

With a tax-favored invest-ment, the earnings (inter-est, dividends, and capital gains) are not taxed until withdrawn.

Hopefully, saving for retirement is one of your main financial goals. The tax code provides several **tax-favored** retirement plan options. A common feature of these options is that the earnings grow tax-deferred from year to year. That's important over time because it allows the earnings to compound at a higher effective rate. Here are the general retirement planning principles you might find useful:

- **It's never too early—and often not too late—to start.** The sooner you put money away, the more time it has to grow.
- **Retirement tax planning is important enough and complicated enough that you should consider meeting with a financial advisor who can help you tailor a personalized plan.**
- **Unless you're approaching age fifty-nine and a half, consider money in-vested in a tax-favored retirement plan to be a long-term investment.**

If your employer matches some or all of your contributions to a retirement account, consider contributing enough to maximize the employer match.

Below, we've offered a general description of some of the more common tax-favored plans.

Individual Retirement Arrangements (IRAs)—Investing in an IRA can be a good idea, even if your contributions aren't deductible. You have to begin taking distributions from a traditional IRA when you reach age seventy and a half. The earnings in your IRA will grow tax-deferred until you decide to withdraw them. If you invest in a traditional IRA, you may be able to deduct all or a portion of your contributions. Generally, distributions from traditional IRAs are partially or fully taxable.

Roth IRAs—A Roth IRA differs from a traditional IRA in several ways: Contributions to a Roth IRA are never deductible; qualified distributions (both contributions and earnings) are entirely tax-free if you take them at least five full years after you first established a Roth IRA *and* after you reach fifty-nine and a half (or if you are disabled, die, or use the distribution for certain first-time home-purchase expenses); and you don't have to take distributions from a Roth IRA when you reach age seventy and a half.

Nonqualified distributions (generally those before age fifty-nine and a half) first come from amounts that have already been taxed, so even a nonqualified distribution may not be taxable.

401(k) Plans—A section 401(k) plan is a qualified retirement plan under which an employee may elect to contribute a portion of his or her wages to the plan. The contributions reduce his or her taxable salary by the amount contributed. These contributions are tax-deferred until they are withdrawn. In addition, the investment income on these deferrals grows tax-deferred until it is withdrawn. Most 401(k) plans allow employees to choose from a wide variety of investment options to match the investor's goals and preferences.

403(b) Plans—Employees of public schools and certain tax-exempt organizations are eligible to participate in tax-sheltered annuity (TSA) plans, also known as 403(b) plans. Eligible employers include nonprofit or charitable organizations and other public interest–oriented organizations, such as universities. Similar to a 401(k), a TSA can provide for employee contributions as well as employer contributions. The tax advantages of a 403(b) plan are similar to those of a 401(k) plan, with contributions and investment earnings growing tax-deferred until withdrawn.

Annuities—When you buy an annuity, you pay for it either with one lump sum or a series of regular premium payments over time. At some point, the annuity makes regular payments back to you. Depending on the annuity, payments can start immediately or can be deferred to allow more money to accumulate. Taxes are deferred until payments begin. Payments can continue for your lifetime (or the lifetime of a beneficiary). An annuity can be either fixed or variable, depending on how it earns income.

If you are considering buying an annuity for income, you'll need to decide whether you want income immediately, and whether you want a guaranteed return that never changes. If you want instant income, purchase what's called an "immediate annuity." Typically, you buy it by making one large payment called a "single premium." People often use immediate annuities (sometimes called "income annuities") as an alternative to using an IRA for lump-sum distributions from an employer plan. When payments are taken, the remaining money continues to earn on a tax-deferred basis, so people often buy them to preserve that tax shelter while receiving income.

If you don't want your income payments to start immediately, you can buy a deferred annuity—so-called because you're postponing the income. Typically, a deferred annuity can be purchased with premiums paid regularly over a period of time or paid as a lump sum. For more information about annuities as investments, see Chapter 8.

If you want a guaranteed return, purchase a "fixed" annuity, which guarantees regular payments of a specific amount. A fixed annuity can be purchased for a specific amount of time or for your lifetime.

Alternatively, you could purchase a "variable" annuity, which pays a return that varies depending upon how the money was invested. Generally they offer investors the option of investing the money in a stock mutual fund, a bond mutual fund, a fixed-rate investment, or a combination.

When Do You Want to Stop Working?

Before you can reach a goal, you need to set it. Decide when you want to retire, and then start working toward that goal. If you hope to retire early, you'd better bring some serious money. You won't get any Social Security before you're sixty-two, and, even then, you'll receive 20 to 30 percent less than if you wait. The longer you work and wait, the more Social Security benefits you'll earn. But if you're able to raise a sizable retirement fund through savings and investments, you may not be as concerned about Social Security.

Also consider the effects of inflation. You may think your nest egg will be sufficient, but prices will go up substantially over a twenty- to thirty-year period after you retire, and that could put a real crimp into your budget.

WHEN CAN YOU COLLECT SOCIAL SECURITY?	
IF YOU WERE BORN IN:	YOU CAN'T COLLECT FULL SOCIAL SECURITY BENEFITS UNTIL AGE:
1937 or earlier	65
1938	65 and 2 months
1939	65 and 4 months
1940	65 and 6 months
1941	65 and 8 months
1942	65 and 10 months
1943-1954	66
1955	66 and 2 months
1956	66 and 4 months
1957	66 and 6 months
1958	66 and 8 months
1959	66 and 10 months
1960 and later	67

Source: Social Security Administration

Magic Birthdays

Generally, there are some birthdays to keep in mind as you approach retirement:

55—The age at which you can begin to use employer plan money without penalty if you terminate employment and the plan is still with your employer.

59½—The age when you're permitted to take distributions from retirement plans such as 401(k)s, profit-sharing plans, thrift plans, and IRAs without paying a penalty. You may still have to pay income taxes on the distributions.

62—The earliest age at which you can begin collecting Social Security. Also, you may qualify for an FHA reverse mortgage to provide income.

65—The age by which you must make your choices about, and sign up for, Medicare.

70½—The age marking when you MUST start withdrawing from IRAs (except for Roth IRAs), and generally from employer-provided retirement plans.

Handling Your Retirement Income

Timing may not be everything, but it can play a crucial role in your long-term retirement income. The timing of when you stop contributing to retirement sources and start receiving payments can have a significant impact on the amount of money you will receive as you progress through your retirement years. Early retirement may seem like a wonderful idea, but it can cost you dearly. If you wait until you're sixty-five or older, you'll make more money—both while you're working and after you retire.

Adjusting Your Budget in Retirement

Your spending patterns may change in retirement as follows.

Things you may spend less on:
- **Clothes**
- **Education**
- **Food**
- **Housing**
- **Life insurance**

Things you may spend more on:
- **Entertainment**
- **Health care**
- **Medical and long-term care insurance**
- **Travel**

Benefits of Working Longer

Here are some factors to consider before you hand in your resignation and decide to retire early:

More Social Security—Generally, the longer you work and contribute to Social Security, the larger your payments will be when you finally do start collecting. If you stop work in your fifties (and stop paying into Social Security), you'll receive considerably less in monthly payments every year from the first year through the end of your life. Over a twenty- to thirty-year period, that could make a significant difference.

On the other hand, if you continue to work until you're sixty-five or seventy, you will receive a larger monthly Social Security payment and could end up with a larger total pay out. Unless you're wealthy and set for life, voluntarily retiring in your fifties might be a financially unwise decision. It could cost you thousands of dollars in long-term retirement payments.

More Pension—Your right to choose when and how to take your pension may be limited by your company. But the longer you work, the more you'll build up in pension payments—and, presumably, the more you'll save while you're still working. Few pension plans provide for a cost-of-living increase after retirement, so the longer you can work and build up pension benefits, the better off you'll be in retirement.

smart step

Start Now!

Calculate how fast your retirement funds can grow.

Log on to
hrblock.com/advisor

Carefully review the statement you should receive annually from the Social Security administration. It predicts how large your Social Security benefits will be and can help you plan your retirement budget.

THE BENEFITS OF POSTPONING SOCIAL SECURITY UNTIL AGE SEVENTY	
IF YOU WERE BORN IN:	**YOUR SOCIAL SECURITY CHECK WILL BE HIGHER BY:**
1929–1930	4.5% per year
1931–1932	5.0% per year
1933–1934	5.5% per year
1935–1936	6.0% per year
1937–1938	6.5% per year
1939–1940	7.0% per year
1941–1942	7.5% per year
1943 or later	8.0% per year

Source: Social Security Administration

Another crucial question regarding your pension is whether to take it in monthly payments or in one lump sum. Most traditional pensions only offer regular payments, but some are more flexible. When you near retirement, sit down with your company's pension administrator and review your options.

Benefits from most traditional pension plans are insured by the federal Pension Benefit Guaranty Corporation, so there is some protection against your benefits disappearing if your company goes into bankruptcy. Check with your employer to see if your plan is covered; if it's not, taking a lump sum might be your only protection against unforeseen circumstances down the road.

If you prefer the security of monthly payments, you may have one other option to consider. Some pension plans offer to continue to pay your spouse after your death, but you may have to accept smaller payments in the meantime in exchange for that benefit. Again, sit down with the pension administrator well before you retire to compare options—lump sum, a standard payout, or a

TAKING YOUR PENSION		
	LUMP SUM	**MONTHLY PAYMENTS**
ADVANTAGES	▪ You have greater control over how the money is invested. ▪ If your company goes bankrupt, your benefits aren't affected. ▪ The possibility for income to stay ahead of inflation exists.	▪ You can choose to have payments go to your spouse after you die. ▪ You have more certainty about your monthly income.
DISADVANTAGES	▪ Investing success or failure is your responsibility. ▪ You can't necessarily count on a specific amount of income. ▪ The possibility of exhausting your pension money exists.	▪ If payments cover a surviving spouse, you will receive smaller payments during your lifetime. ▪ Unless they're adjusted for inflation, pension payments will lose buying power over time. ▪ You may be able to protect your spouse or provide regular monthly payments in other ways.

lifetime pension for your spouse—and figure out which option would make the most sense for you. Safety should be a key concern.

Steep Health Care Costs—Health care expenses can consume a sizeable portion of a retiree's income—even for those with Medicare. For retirees without Medicare, health care can take up even more. Health insurance from your employer is usually cheaper than other options. However, an increasing number

of companies are dropping health care coverage for retirees, so don't underestimate its value when planning the timing of your retirement. In fact, you may
need to work a couple of extra years just to make up for the additional health
insurance you'll have to pay once you retire.

Access to Retirement Savings—There are two key timing issues with your
retirement account savings: When you *can* start taking money out, and when
you *must* start taking money out. Once you reach age fifty-nine and a half, you
can begin to take money out of any tax-deferred retirement plans without paying a penalty. If you're still working, there would be no point in taking money
out. In fact, it's a good idea to continue contributing to your tax-deferred savings plans as long as possible.

If you maxed out your contributions to tax-favored plans while you were working and were still able to put money into a taxable account, tap into the taxable
account first. Because you've already paid taxes on money you put into a taxable
account, and have paid taxes on the earnings annually, you won't owe tax on
any money you withdraw. In the meantime, your 401(k) or IRA account can continue to grow tax-deferred.

If you don't need any money from your retirement account, you can continue to
keep the money growing tax-deferred in that account until you reach age seventy and a half. Then, you have to start withdrawing the money and paying
taxes on the withdrawals. If that's your biggest worry—being forced to start taking some of your money out of a retirement plan at age seventy and a half—you
should have a great retirement.

Turning Retirement Savings into Income

If you don't need to start using your tax-deferred money, consider rolling part or all of a lump sum into a traditional IRA. You continue to postpone paying taxes on the money, but after fifty-nine and a half, you can withdraw money from the account as you need it without any additional penalty.

If you were born before 1936 and receive your employment-related retirement assets in a lump sum, you may be able to use a tax computation called ten-year averaging, and it has the potential to save you a lot of money. Essentially, you pay tax on the entire **distribution** when you receive it, but at a lower rate than your marginal rate. But using this method is complicated, and it may or may not be your best option. Consult your tax professional about ten-year averaging *before* you take the distribution.

If you've reached age seventy and a half, you'll need to figure out what your minimum required distribution (MRD) is for both your employer plan and your traditional IRAs. The government wants all your tax-deferred money to be out of these accounts by the time you die, so they require you to set up a withdrawal schedule for each one.

The amount of your annual MRD is a function of the amount in your account and your age in the year of the distribution. A married individual whose spouse is more than ten years younger may figure MRDs taking into account the spouse's age. This choice reduces the amount of the MRDs, allowing additional tax deferral. The rules are confusing, but luckily the custodian of your account can usually make them for you. If you must determine your MRD yourself, seek professional assistance.

If you don't take at least this amount every year after you turn seventy and a half, you'll be assessed a 50 percent penalty on the gap between your MRD and

plain talk

A distribution is money taken out of a tax-deferred retirement plan, such as a 401(k) or IRA.

the amount you actually withdrew. For example, if your MRD was $12,000 and you only took out $10,000, you would pay a $1,000 penalty—half of the $2,000 difference.

Minimum required distributions don't apply to Roth IRAs. You never have to withdraw money from a Roth IRA, so take money from a Roth IRA only if you need it.

Retirement Money Before You Retire

One of the big drawbacks of a tax-deferred retirement account is that you generally face a 10 percent penalty if you withdraw the money before age fifty-nine and a half. But if you find yourself in financial straits, you may have to tap into your retirement money.

There are certain circumstances under which you may borrow from your retirement plan account without paying a penalty. But be careful about taking out money as a loan. If you leave your company for any reason, your loan must generally be paid back in full. Otherwise, you'll pay the same penalties and taxes that you would have with a straight withdrawal. If you're totally disabled, you will face no withdrawal penalty, and if you die, your heirs will not be charged a penalty for withdrawing the money from your account.

Finally, if you're fifty-five or older and you leave your employer, you can avoid an early withdrawal penalty from your employer's plan if you set up a schedule to withdraw money periodically over at least five years (it doesn't have to be the full amount). You can use the money to help pay for such items as college tuition, alimony, child support, or even your month-to-month expenses. But there are some restrictions, so it's best to seek professional help when setting up a withdrawal plan.

THE CHALLENGE

Gordon and Mary, both age sixty, are concerned about their retirement savings. Recent stock market declines have cut the amount in their 401(k) plans by about a third. "With our kids out of college and on their own, we thought we could retire in a couple of years, but now we're not sure," said Mary. "We've been pretty frugal all our lives, but now it looks like we'll be working for quite a while yet," added Gordon.

THE PLAN

Gordon and Mary made an appointment with a financial advisor. The first thing the advisor did was to ask the couple to prepare a net worth statement. "What a pleasant surprise that was," said Mary. "When we added up all our savings and investments from over the years, it turned out we were worth a lot more than we thought." "Still," added Gordon, "we're not quite there yet financially, but it looks like we can be with two or three more years of hard work." The advisor also suggested that for the years they remain working, both Gordon and Mary continue to contribute the allowable maximums to their 401(k) plans. He also suggested opening and contributing the maximum amount to Roth IRAs. She pointed out that distributions from the Roth IRAs will be tax-free, and that if they don't need the money, there are no mandatory withdrawals at age seventy and a half, as there are with traditional IRAs.

"The advisor also suggested we consider purchasing an annuity with one of our 401(k) plans when we retire. The annuity would pay us a monthly income and, along with our Social Security benefits, would provide a steady income for the rest of our lives," said Gordon. "We feel better knowing that with a bit more effort we can have the retirement lifestyle we want," said Mary.

IRAs carry the same penalties for early withdrawals as 401(k) plans, with some exceptions. However, unlike a 401(k) plan, you can't borrow from an IRA.

Before you withdraw any money from your retirement account, however, make sure it's an act of last resort. This is money you *will* need later—possibly more than you need it now.

Whether you decide to work after retirement or hit the links—or both—the sooner you start to research and weigh your options, the more control you're likely to have over the second stage of your life.

the ESSENTIALS

1 Get an early start planning and investing for retirement.

2 The age at which you retire will permanently affect your Social Security benefits; the sooner you take benefits, the lower they'll be.

3 The more dependent you think you'll be on Social Security benefits, the more you might want to think about postponing retirement to increase their value.

4 Saving for retirement should be one of your main financial goals. Unless you are close to retirement, try to think of your retirement-related investments as long-term investments. Don't access the money early if at all possible.

5 Retirement planning is important and complicated enough to consider consulting a professional advisor.

11 [DISASTERS AND DELIGHTS: Coping with Life's Unexpected Situations]

"I'm not afraid of storms, for I'm learning to sail my ship."

—Louisa May Alcott

ife rarely goes according to plan. If you survive forty-five years of uninter-rupted employment and retire at sixty-five with pension and profit sharing, congratulations! You can move on to the fly-fishing books, gardening, or whatever else your retirement dream involves. Mergers, acquisitions, bankrupt-cies, and corporate downsizing have made job stability a thing of the past. In other words, this is not your father's economy.

There's a good chance that in your lifetime, you will be fired, laid off, or other-wise lose your job to a corporate bankruptcy, merger, or acquisition   as millions of Americans learned during the economic downturn over the last few years.

Setbacks can also happen in your personal life. A long-term injury or illness could cut dramatically into your savings plans. So could an unexpected baby. If you're married, there's about a 50 percent chance that you'll eventually get divorced. You have to be prepared to deal with a variety of personal and finan-cial setbacks over the course of your life.

Fortunately, not every unexpected change in your life will be for the worse. You might get a better job, a promotion, or a raise. You might get a windfall from a relative. You might hit it big in the stock market, or win the lottery. Your chil-dren might get full-ride scholarships. How you adapt to the curves life throws you will go a long way in determining how successful you'll be in preparing for a prosperous retirement.

If the unexpected event is negative rather than positive, you can weather the storm financially if you're prepared. With so much uncertainty surrounding your financial life, your first priority should be to put away enough cash for a safety net. Earlier in the book, we stressed the importance of establishing an emer-gency fund for the unexpected. If you can put aside enough money assets to cover your expenses for three to six months, you should be able to weather most financial setbacks

Money and Divorce

D ivorce is one of the most traumatic and emotional events during a person's lifetime—particularly for those with children. While the emotional aspects of divorce can be devastating, there are financial consequences as well. Even an emergency fund cannot cover the potential economic impact on the people involved.

If you think you might be heading for divorce, here are some steps that can help you manage its economic impact:

- **Build your own separate credit record.** Establish an independent credit record while you're married. If divorce occurs, you'll have some financial credibility with lenders if you need to borrow money.
- **Close out any joint bank or credit card accounts.** If one party defaults, it will ruin the credit record for both spouses, even if the court says only one party is responsible for the debt. Get new credit cards in your own name, and open an individual bank account.
- **Pay off credit card debt in advance.** List all debts so they can be assigned to one of you or divided.
- **Take an inventory of your financial situation.** Get yourself organized by making a list of all assets (joint and separate), including such things as bank and brokerage accounts, investments and retirement savings plans, and property, such as a home, cars, collections, antiques, furnishings, and jewelry.
- **Locate key documents.** This includes tax returns for the past several years, insurance policies, IRA and pension statements, and estate planning documents.

If divorce is inevitable:

- **Use a mediator.** Try to reach an agreement on key issues involving the split-up, such as custody of children and pets, and the division of property. Mediation is not only less expensive than going through the court system, it also

smart step

Review your financial plan whenever you experience significant life changes, such as a job change, family additions, divorce, or marriage, but at least on an annual basis.

If you've expe-
rience a life
event, like mar-
riage, divorce,
or dependent
changes, make
sure that the
beneficiary
arrangements
for all your
insurance and
investment
products agree
with your will.

helps you focus on potential solutions instead of battling over the marital differences. Once those issues are resolved, attorneys can review the mediation
agreement and draw up the formal documents. This approach will cost less
both in time and money.

- **Don't forget to include pension and Social Security benefits as part of
  your joint assets, even if you were not the working partner.** If you are
  listed as the beneficiary on your spouse's 401(k) or IRA, you may be asked to
  waive your rights as part of the settlement.
- **Document everything you can.** Include the need for alimony or child support, your hard work putting your spouse through school, and any property
  you owned separately before or during the marriage. Gather information
  about your spouse's salary, stock options, and the like.
- **If you've been covered by your spouse's health insurance, line up another carrier and get your own policy started before you are taken off
  your spouse's policy.**

After the divorce:

- **Check to make sure your credit report is accurate and has not been affected by any of the divorce complications.**
- **Change beneficiaries on your IRAs, 401(k) or 403(b) plans, pensions,
  insurance policies, and will.** If you don't currently have a will, make one.
- **Change the title on any property that has changed hands, such as a
  home or automobile.**
- **Review your insurance to see if your coverage needs have changed.**
- **Review your tax situation.** If you receive alimony, it's taxable, but if you pay
  it, it's tax deductible. Child support, however, is neither deductible if you pay
  it, nor taxable if you receive it on behalf of your children. Generally, the custodial parent can take the dependency exemptions for the children, but that parent is allowed to waive the exemption to the noncustodial parent. We suggest
  you talk to your tax professional or legal advisor about your particular tax situ-

ation *before* negotiating the terms of your divorce. It's important to know in advance the tax implications of certain agreements. In addition, that knowledge might provide you with a negotiating edge.

- **If you remarry, and you want to leave assets to your children from a prior marriage, you may want to put your assets in your own name.** Otherwise, your assets may automatically pass on to your new spouse, who then might pass your money on to his or her children instead of yours. As an alternative, you could also set up a plan in which your spouse can use your money for living expenses until he or she dies, at which time it is passed on to your children.

Career Changes

Colleges have been telling graduates for years that it's not "if" you lose your job, but "when." Job security is a foreign concept in today's economy, so you must be prepared for the worst. If you were to lose your job, would you have the financial resources to sustain you and your family through a lengthy job search?

You need a strong financial foundation to face any type of adversity—and a job search is no exception. You don't want to go into a job interview in desperate financial straits. You'll be too likely to settle for the first offer rather than to hold out for something more appropriate.

If you fear that your job could be in jeopardy, here are some steps to take right now to bolster your financial foundation:

- **Build up your short-term assets.** That three- to six-month emergency safety net could come in handy if you lose your job. Try to pad the savings a little more.

If you're having trouble dividing certain assets—for example, a home—or you don't want to sell it now, a third party may find alternative ways to calculate value or substitute assets.

Update your re-
sumé regularly
so you'll be pre-
pared when
opportunities
(job offers) or
challenges (lay-
offs) come your
way.

- **Stop spending.** Cut out everything you don't truly need—a new car, appli-
ances, clothing, entertainment, meals out, premium cable stations, even vacations. Put everything on hold. If you were planning a trip, cancel it. It's
impossible to really enjoy a vacation when you're out of work anyway. Once you
find a job, try to negotiate the vacation back into the job offer. When you're offered a job, mention that you had a family vacation planned for a particular
week. The new employer may let you take that time off. If they've already decided to hire you, they may accommodate your reasonable special requests.

- **Do your best to pay off all consumer debts and credit cards while
you're still working.** The fewer payments you have to make, the farther your
savings will take you.

- **Set up a home equity line of credit.** The worst time to borrow money is
when you're out of work. It's best to get one step ahead of the game. If you
own your own home, set up a home equity line of credit while you're still
working. With a line of credit, you don't pay for any points and you won't owe
any interest if you don't borrow from the account. But if you do get laid off,
have a line of credit to fall back on if your savings start to dwindle.

- **Learn about your employer's severance policy.** If you're entitled to severance pay, determine what you'll receive if you're laid off.

- **Get an extra credit card.** Worst-case scenario, it could be months before you
find another job. You may need all the financial resources you can lay your
hands on to get you through. While you're working you should have no problem lining up a good credit card with a relatively low interest rate as an emergency financial back-up.

- **Use up any money in employer-provided child care or health care
spending accounts.** You won't be able to roll it over.

- **Get your resume ready and start researching the job market.** If you do
lose your job, the sooner you can find another, the sooner you can get back on
track with your financial plan.

The Pink Slip—If the day finally comes when you lose your job, there are several tasks to take care of immediately:

- **Try to negotiate a better severance package, as well as additional help to find another job.** Don't be shy about asking for more than your company's first offer—what are they going to do, fire you? Ask for the continuation of health benefits for a longer period. If you feel that the company has not offered a suitable severance package, talk to a lawyer who specializes in employee matters, and see if it is worth pursuing a larger settlement.

- **Don't give up your medical insurance.** COBRA (Consolidated Omnibus Budget Reconciliation Act) provisions allow you to continue coverage with your current insurer for eighteen months after you leave the company, although you'll pay most or all of the premiums yourself. Have another policy ready to go when the company policy ends. You don't want to be without health insurance.

- **File for unemployment benefits immediately.** Benefits may take a while to start and you may be eligible even if you receive a severance package.

- **If you have any debt, you may want to talk to your lender about reducing or deferring payments or interest**. Tell the creditor that you've lost your job but that you're actively looking for employment. You may be able to work out alternative payment arrangements.

- **If your old company requires you to remove your balance in your retirement plan, have your former employer roll it directly into an IRA.** Use a separate IRA account from your other IRA money. That may allow you to put it into your new employer's plan later if you wish.

- **If money gets tight, you may have to withdraw money from your IRA, but make that a last resort.** That money is earmarked for your retirement. Besides, you may have to pay income taxes on the taxable portion of the withdrawal as well as a 10 percent penalty (unless you're over fifty-nine and a half or meet the requirements for one of several other exceptions to the penalty).

- **Consider putting at least some nonretirement money in investments focused on protecting the immediate value of your money.** For example, you may want to put it into a money market account instead of stocks.

smart step

Don't pay a penalty on early withdrawals from your IRA until you talk to a tax professional. There are several exceptions to the penalty, and you may be able to claim one.

Medical Maladies

An accident or illness could severely hamper the best financial plans. If you or a member of your family should suffer a serious illness or injury, would you be prepared? Before a medical emergency strikes your family, make sure that your medical coverage is adequate. Consider buying disability insurance if you aren't covered at work or if your employer's coverage is inadequate.

There are several steps you need to take immediately if you have serious medical problems on the home front.

- **Find out more about the illness.** Research it at the library or online, and talk to the doctor to find out as much as possible. Not only will that give you a clearer idea of what to expect from the medical condition, it will also help you prepare financially.
- **If the illness is terminal, make sure the will, durable powers of attorney, and related matters are in order.** Make sure the beneficiaries on pensions, IRAs, 401(k) plans, insurance policies, and **durable power of attorney** documents are up-to-date and accurate.
- **If you or your spouse has a disability policy, review it immediately and contact the insurance company to let it know about the situation.** Find out when benefits would start, how much income they would provide, and whether or not they're taxable.
- **Contact Social Security to see when you or your spouse might qualify for disability benefits.** The requirements are tough and benefits typically take several months to kick in, but many Americans with long-term injuries receive Social Security payments for months or years.
- **Let your creditors know of your situation.** You may be able to work out alternative payment arrangements.
- **Review your budget to adjust for medical costs.** If you're considering withdrawing money from a retirement account or selling an investment to

cover your extra costs, consult your tax professional or investment advisor to see if there are better options to consider.

- **If the ailment is terminal, see if your life insurance policy might provide accelerated benefits or a viatical settlement that can be used while the insured person is still alive.** You may have to pay taxes on the payments. The buyer will continue to pay the premiums, and will receive the insurance benefits after your death.
- **Consider shifting some of your long-term investment dollars into more liquid short-term accounts so that you have easy access to the money if you need it.**

However, if you have a family, use your life insurance money only as a last resort. That insurance is earmarked to help your family pay the bills after you're gone.

Death of a Loved One—The death of a loved one is traumatic. However, even when you're dealing with the emotional upheaval of an imminent death, you still need to focus on the financial ramifications. Here are a few steps to take:

- **Consider a pre-need funeral contract, which can ease the financial and emotional burden for survivors.** These contracts can cover a wide variety of services and will ease the financial burden for your spouse or dependents.
- **Get professional advice about estate planning and how to minimize probate and tax problems for any heirs.** Make sure both partners have a working relationship with your financial advisor, and that both know where all the important documents, including wills, health care proxies, and durable powers of attorney, are located.
- **Make a complete, up-to-date list of all assets.** The executor will need the information to process the will. If there are any assets you do not want to go through probate, make sure they're held jointly with your spouse. (Life insurance proceeds and money in an IRA also do not go through probate.)

plain talk

If you are terminally ill, you may be able to sell your life insurance policy to a third party in exchange for a lump sum of money while you are still alive. This is called a viatical settlement.

- Have your attorney review the will so it can be submitted for probate if necessary.
- Make copies of your marriage certificate in order to apply for spousal benefits.
- If you plan to apply for Social Security benefits, you'll need your children's birth certificates.

Handling a Death in the Family—If your spouse dies, once again you'll have more than just the emotional distress to deal with. There are a number of steps you need to take as soon as possible:

- Get multiple certified copies of the death certificate.
- Notify the issuers of any life insurance policies as soon as possible so claims processing can get underway quickly.
- Apply for death or survivor benefits from Social Security, Medicare, the Veterans Administration, a union, pension, or annuity. You may need a copy of all or any of the following: the deceased's death certificate, marriage certificate, birth certificates (including those of your children), military discharge papers, Social Security number, will, a list of assets, and the most recent tax return.
- Check with Social Security before depositing any Social Security checks issued to the deceased.
- Notify all retirement or investment accounts of which you are the beneficiary.
- Change all joint financial institution and credit card accounts into your name alone.
- Review your investment strategy to ensure that it still makes sense. Don't feel pressured to make major changes, such as selling a home, immediately.
- Review your insurance to see if anything needs to be changed.
- Contact current or previous employers to see if you're entitled to any survivor's pension benefits.

THE CHALLENGE

About six months ago, Leah's husband died, leaving Leah, age forty-five, and her fifteen-year-old daughter emotionally, but not financially, devastated. Leah's husband had maintained life insurance coverage for $500,000. "Fortunately, we didn't have to worry about our finances while we grieved," Leah said. "I knew I'd need to properly invest the money eventually, but at first I just put it all in a money market account with my broker. In the meantime, my teacher's salary was enough to keep us going."

THE PLAN

When Leah's life resumed some semblance of normalcy, she met with her financial advisor several times to discuss what to do with the $500,000 from her husband's life insurance. "I want my daughter to be able to attend college without worrying about money, and I want a safe retirement, but I didn't know exactly how to make those things happen," said Leah. After considerable thought, Leah decided on the following allocation of her assets.

- She left $30,000 in the money market fund for emergencies.
- She invested $60,000 in a section 529 plan to make sure her daughter could attend the college of her choice.
- She put $100,000 in an insured annuity, with monthly payments to start when Leah retires.

- She used $50,000 to pay off the remaining mortgage on her home.
- She used $5,000 to pay off credit card debts and some leftover debt from her husband's funeral.
- She donated $15,000 to her synagogue to fund a revolving scholarship for teens in the congregation.
- She put $230,000 in a diversified investment portfolio consisting of blue-chip stocks and highly rated corporate bonds.
- She took $10,000 to fund a summer trip to the Far East, something she and her daughter had been wanting to do for several years.

"With this allocation, I felt both my daughter's education and my retirement were secure, and I was able to do some extra things with part of the money as well," Leah said.

- See if you need to change the titles on any property, such as a home or car.
- If your will named your deceased spouse, it will need updating.

Dealing with a Windfall

I t may come as a large inheritance, a bonus from work, a gain on your stock, or a lottery jackpot, but if fortune smiles on you, you want to make the most of your financial windfall.

Windfalls can come and go at a dizzying pace. Lottery winners, professional athletes, famous entertainers, and millionaire entrepreneurs have all been known to squander their fortunes through free spending and poor investment decisions. Don't let it happen to you. Should you ever be lucky enough to receive a windfall, take care of your long-term financial needs first. Easy come, easy go is no way to treat your financial windfall.

Here are some steps to safeguard your newfound fortune:

- **Put the money in a safe place—a money market bank account, for instance—while you sort out your options.**
- **See your tax professional to learn how taxes may have an impact on your payout.** If you have options for receiving the money (such as a lump sum or periodic payments), figure out which option would minimize your tax liability and maximize your investment opportunities.
- **Talk with your financial advisor to determine the best way to invest your assets to provide a balance of safety and return.** You may want to consider investing some of your assets in real estate and stocks.
- **Shift a large portion of your assets into tax-deferred retirement plans.** You might also put some money into a lump-sum annuity that can grow tax-deferred until you draw out the money.

- **Don't start spending money on high-dollar impulse purchases such as boats and big-screen TV sets unless you're sure your children's college funds are covered and your retirement program is properly funded.** Given the chance, you can spend a lot of money in a short amount of time. Put away enough money to cover all of the essentials in the years ahead—compensating for inflation—before you start spending.
- **Set up an estate plan to specify where your money will go when you die.** If you already have an estate plan, you may want to review it.
- **If your windfall is known to others, you may soon receive requests for money from various organizations.** It's also possible you'll hear from relatives, friends, and acquaintances who need gifts or loans. Resist these pleas for the time being. When the dust settles, you can make charitable contributions and helping friends and relatives a part of your overall financial plan if that is what you decide.

With a little planning and fiscal restraint, you could turn a financial windfall into a personal expense account that will cover your every need for the rest of your life.

Protecting Your Financial Identity

Identity theft is a growing problem and can be financially devastating to its victims. It can ruin your good name, destroy your personal finances, and wipe out the good credit history you've worked hard to create. Identity theft occurs when personal data such as your Social Security number, credit card numbers, financial account numbers, etc. are used for fraudulent purposes. Once someone has obtained personal data about you, he or she can wreak havoc by doing things like accessing and draining your bank accounts, obtaining loans in your name, purchasing cars, and running up credit card bills. Clearing up this type of problem can be extremely time consuming and very expensive. There are steps you can take to prevent the theft of your identity, including the purchase of identity fraud expense insurance coverage. While insurance won't prevent the fraud, it will assist with certain expenses associated with clearing your name and repairing your financial records.

Here are some easy steps you can take to help keep you from becoming an identity-theft victim:

- **Don't give out personal information over the telephone or Internet unless you are certain of who is requesting it and why disclosing the information is necessary.**
- **Don't leave documents with your personal financial information in your automobile.**
- **Guard your Social Security number and don't use it for other purposes such as for a driver's license number, and don't give it out unless necessary.**
- **If you are discarding documents that contain personal financial information make sure they are fully destroyed, not just thrown in the trash—consider purchasing a shredder.** These documents include old tax returns, account statements, credit card slips, financial solicitations, etc.
- **Only use a secure, official Post Office Collection Box for mailing purposes.**
- **Order and review a copy of your credit report at least annually.**
- **Protect unique passwords and PINs for all accounts and change them regularly.**
- **Remove unnecessary items that contain personal information from your wallet or purse.**
- **Report stolen or lost checks, credit and debit cards immediately.**
- **Review all items on your bills and investigate anything suspicious immediately.**
- **Safeguard your ATM number and receipts.**

Major life changes often have an impact on both your income and estate tax situation. Consult a professional who can advise you on what the changes will be and the options for handling them.

the ESSENTIALS

1 An emergency fund equal to three to six months' expenses is the best way to keep your finances on track should the unexpected hit.

2 Be sure your records are up to date and can be found quickly if an emergency arises.

3 A crisis is no time to be making major life changes, especially those that involve serious financial consequences. Give yourself time to recover from the shock before you make major decisions.

4 After a major change in your personal circumstances, make sure that key information such as beneficiaries, account ownership, and credit records are updated and accurate.

5 Safeguard all of your personal financial information to help prevent the theft of your identity.

12 [PASSING IT ON:
Planning Your Estate]

"When it comes to dividing an estate,
the politest men quarrel."
—Ralph Waldo Emerson

When a person
dies without a
will—known as
dying intestate—
the assets are
disposed of
according to
state law.

Estate planning is not only for the wealthy. Just as you plan your finances during your life, estate planning allows you to decide how your assets will be distributed after you're gone. Of course, you could let the state decide—which is exactly what will happen if you don't set up your own estate plan—but if you have family, friends, or a favorite charity, leaving your estate in the hands of the government may not be the best idea. An estate plan, even a simple one, allows you to dictate the financial arrangements that you believe are best for those you leave behind. Careful estate planning also can mean that your estate may have to pay fewer inheritance taxes.

Preparing an estate plan can be a fairly complex process, but for many people, it's relatively straightforward. Generally, you will need an attorney who specializes in estate planning to draw up some of the important documents, such as wills, trusts, and other estate planning documents to ensure that the documents are legally enforceable.

Estate Planning Essentials

There are several elements to a comprehensive estate plan. Here are the key elements of estate planning:

Will—Everyone needs a will, even those with small estates. In most cases, property passes to a spouse and any children, but the formula for distributing assets varies from state to state. Dying **intestate** can cost far more in taxes, cause legal, bureaucratic, and emotional difficulties for survivors, and ultimately keep the property from going where the deceased person wanted it to go. With a will, you specify exactly how your assets are divided among your family, friends, and favorite charities.

Here are some other important items you can include in your will:

- **Naming a guardian for your children, and an executor to administer the provisions of the will**
- **Distribution of your assets to your heirs and how it should be done such as equal or unequal shares**
- **If some of your heirs are young, at what age they should have access to their share**
- **Leaving specific property to certain heirs**
- **Whether to clearly omit or disinherit any potential heirs**
- **Specific gifts to charities or other organizations**

Titling Assets—One of the most basic estate planning steps is to take title to assets as "joint tenants with right of survivorship." By doing so, at the death of one of the joint tenants, the titled property automatically passes to the surviving tenant(s) without having to go through probate.

Account Beneficiaries—Make sure the proper beneficiaries are listed on your retirement plans, Roth IRAs, traditional IRAs, and insurance policies. The money goes to the beneficiary named on those accounts. Your will does not control the disposition of these assets unless your estate is named as the beneficiary.

General Power of Attorney—This legal document names someone you trust to handle your affairs if you become incapacitated or die. A durable power of attorney takes effect immediately. A springing power of attorney doesn't take effect until you become incapacitated.

Health Care Power of Attorney or Living Will—A health care power of attorney designates someone to make decisions about your medical care if you are unable to do so. If you do not have someone you trust to make such decisions, a living will leaves instructions for your doctor about when to discontinue life support for you if you are in a terminal condition.

Trusts—Trusts can give you more flexibility in passing on your assets. They can also help your estate avoid estate taxes and probate. There's more on trusts later in this chapter.

Lifetime Gifts—Gifts to friends and family during your lifetime can reduce the amount of your assets that is subject to estate tax. For example, in 2003, $11,000 can be transferred to each donee without gift or estate tax consequences.

Charitable Bequests—Property transferred for charitable or public purposes can reduce the taxable value of your estate, thereby reducing the amount of estate taxes. You can donate to qualified charities while you're alive or have assets assigned to charities after your death through your will or through a charitable trust. Your tax deduction will be limited if the trust is a charitable remainder or charitable lead trust. See a tax professional before setting up such a trust.

The Probate Process

Nearly all estates are settled in probate court—even those that include a proper will. But a will should make the probate process quicker and easier. Without a will, your estate could be tied up in probate for years while the court decides how to disburse your assets and, if necessary, appoint a legal guardian for your children. Don't put your family through that nightmare. Spend the time and effort to prepare a valid will.

When you have a valid will, here are the steps the probate process will follow:

- **The court will determine if a will exists, and if it is valid.**
- **The court assigns an executor to administer the estate (the person designated in the will unless the person is unavailable).**

- **The court monitors the executor's efforts to identify assets, pay off debts, and dispose of the remaining money and property to the beneficiaries.** The process can be time-consuming, but the executor may receive compensation in the form of a percentage of the estate (normally 1 to 5 percent).
- **If the court approves the executor's actions, the estate is settled.** Probate can take several months at best, several years at worst.

It's possible to avoid probate, but it takes some extra effort. You can avoid probate if you give away all your assets before you die, but that's probably not reasonable. You could hold your assets in joint tenancy with someone else, in which case the assets go directly to the joint owner(s). But those assets will ultimately go through probate as part of the surviving joint tenant's estate. Or, you can set one or more trusts to hold your money and assets until your death, at which time it goes to the beneficiaries in the terms you set. You can read more on trusts later in this chapter.

For all of its drawbacks, including court costs and attorney's fees, the probate process offers one important benefit. It offers protection from creditors until the estate has been probated and the assets disbursed.

A Taxing Situation

fast fact

Subject to certain limitations, assets that you place into a charitable trust, such as stocks and bonds, may be deducted for income tax purposes for the year of contribution.

Your heirs are not the only ones who will want a piece of your estate when you're gone. Uncle Sam would also like a share. Your job is to minimize that amount as much as possible. You can pass up to $1 million on to anyone tax-free (as of 2003; that limit will increase gradually in the years ahead). After the first $1 million, your estate will be taxed at rate of at least 41 percent—and possibly as high as 49 percent.

smart step

Start Now!

Create your
Net Worth
Worksheet to
help determine
the value of
your estate.

Log on to
hrblock.com/advisor

Here are some steps you can take to minimize the taxes your survivors would pay on your estate:

Give it Away—If you have money to spare, with no fear of running out before you die, you might start giving it away. You can give away up to $11,000 per year (in 2003) per person to whomever you want. If you have three children, for instance, you can give each child $11,000 gift tax-free. Your spouse can also give away up to $11,000 per year per person. So if you have three children, each spouse can give each child $11,000—$22,000 per child—or a total of $66,000 per year, gift tax-free.

Donate to Charity—All the money you donate to charity—either while you're alive or in your will after you're gone—will reduce your total net worth, and therefore will reduce your estate taxes. Charitable donations of any amount can be made without gift tax consequences.

Divide Assets Between Spouses—If you and your spouse have assets of $2 million, you could divide your assets equally, and keep $1 million in your name and $1 million in your spouse's name. That way, when you die, you can each leave that $1 million to your heirs tax-free. There is, however, one problem with that arrangement: When one spouse dies, the surviving spouse would not have the benefit of the other spouse's money and your heirs receive your assets regardless of their age or financial health.

But you can solve that problem with a special trust, known as a "credit shelter trust" or "bypass trust." With a bypass trust, when one spouse dies, his or her assets go into the trust rather than directly to the other spouse or other beneficiaries. Even though the trust would be earmarked for the children or other beneficiaries, the money stays in the trust as long as the surviving spouse lives. That spouse is able to use the income generated by the assets in the trust until he or she dies. The spouse may also have access to the trust principal. When the surviving spouse dies, the money in the trust is passed on to the beneficiaries without further estate tax consequences. The assets of the second spouse to die also pass onto the heirs tax-free up to $1 million. That way, each parent passed on $1 million tax-free to their children (or other beneficiaries)—a total of $2 million in all.

Setting up a trust to avoid inheritance taxes may seem like a lot of work, but consider this: If parents leave a lump sum of $2 million, the heirs would get the first $1,565,000, and $435,000 goes to estate taxes. That's no small sum. So the effort to set up a credit shelter trust can pay off in a big way.

Creating a Trust

Trusts can offer a number of benefits, in addition to alleviating estate taxes. A trust can help manage the estate's assets for the benefit of those who inherit it, help support children who are too young or otherwise unable to care for themselves, and assets held in the trust generally avoid probate. Trusts are not something you should set up on your own. The assistance of a knowledgeable attorney can be invaluable.

Trusts can serve you and your family in a number of ways. As stated previously, one of the best advantages is keeping your assets out of the probate process. Assets held in trusts can go to heirs quickly and easily—unless you choose to keep them in the trust. By setting up a trust during your lifetime, you can avoid subjecting your assets to public scrutiny.

A trust may be either revocable or irrevocable.

- **Revocable trusts.** These trusts can be changed or canceled after they're set up, while irrevocable trusts cannot. With a revocable trust, the money in the

smart step

Obtain competent professional help when creating a trust. There are many types of trusts to choose from and many legal standards that must be met.

One thing that
a living trust
can't do is
reduce your
estate taxes.
However, provi-
sions in the
trust document
can include
a credit shelter
trust, charitable
transfers, and
other estate
planning
choices.

trust is considered part of your estate when you die. You would pay income taxes on the revenue generated within the trust as if no trust existed.

- **Irrevocable trusts.** These trusts will not be part of your estate to the extent that you did not retain an interest in the trust (grantor trust).

There are several other types of trusts that could offer benefits for your estate plan:

Living Grantor Trust—As the name suggests, a living trust allows you to keep your assets in a trust while you are living. Known also as a revocable inter vivos trust, or a grantor trust, this type of trust offers several unique features. While you're alive, you can name yourself as the trustee of the trust, and manage the assets yourself. Once you die, the trust immediately becomes a "regular" trust and its assets are handled according to the trust document. By placing most of your assets in a living trust, you can simplify your will and minimize the portion of your estate subject to probate.

QTIP Trust—Short for "qualified terminable interest property" trust, a QTIP trust is similar to a bypass trust except that it qualifies for unlimited marital deduction and avoids estate taxes upon the death of the first spouse. With a QTIP trust, all the income generated by the trust goes to your surviving spouse. When your spouse dies, the money in the trust would be passed on to your children (or other beneficiaries). Assets in the QTIP trust at the time of the second-to-die spouse's death are included in that spouse's estate and thus, possibly subject to estate taxes.

Irrevocable Life Insurance Trust (ILIT)—With an irrevocable life insurance trust, your life insurance policy belongs to the trust. If you want delayed payments for your children, for instance, that can be stipulated in the trust. The good thing is that because the insurance proceeds belong to the trust, proceeds

THE CHALLENGE

John's health is failing and it appears his wife, Sally, will live many years beyond his death. John wants to provide for Sally, but he also wants to pass his estate on to his three children from a previous marriage. He does not want any of his assets to pass to Sally's children. How can John make sure Sally is taken care of throughout her life while still passing his assets on to his children?

THE PLAN

John may choose to set up a QTIP trust that will pay the trust income to Sally for her life, with the assets in the trust going to John's children upon Sally's death. One "catch" here is that Sally's estate will include the assets that are in the QTIP trust at the time of her death. Any estate tax paid on those assets will reduce the amount of assets that pass to John's children. Also, if *all* of John's assets go to the QTIP trust, his estate will pay no estate taxes, but his estate tax exemption will be wasted. John's children may have to wait thirty years or longer before they can enjoy any of their inheritance.

To avoid the pitfalls of the QTIP trust, a non-QTIP trust could be set up. In this case, the trust document could provide for Sally's needs, but also allow distributions to John's children during the life of the trust, if John so desires. John's estate will pay tax on the assets that go to this trust, but the assets will escape further estate tax when Sally dies.

Depending on the size of John's assets, he may choose to set up both a QTIP trust and a non-QTIP trust. The QTIP trust would provide income to Sally until her death, but because it's funded with only part of John's estate, estate tax consequences upon Sally's death can be minimized. The second trust could provide distributions to Sally if her financial needs are not being met by the QTIP trust and any other provisions that John wished to include.

Plan your own funeral and burial. While it may be difficult, you'll save your grieving survivors time, trouble, and expense by picking out and paying for the burial plot, the marker, and the funeral.

are not added to your taxable estate, nor does the money need to pass through probate. The insurance proceeds can be used for such things as paying debts of the estate or paying estate taxes, and the remainder is disbursed under terms of the trust document.

Standby Trust—A standby trust becomes active only upon the occurrence of a specific event, usually disability of the trust creator (grantor). The trust is only minimally funded until the trustee (usually a bank) is notified that the grantor has become incapacitated. If the grantor dies before the assets are gathered into the trust, the trust is wasted.

Spendthrift Trust—If you have a son, daughter, or other beneficiary who has had a history of spending problems, you can set up a special trust known as a spendthrift trust that protects trust income and assets from the beneficiary's creditors. Certain creditors, such as the U.S. government, are not affected by spendthrift provisions.

Charitable Remainder Trust—There is a trust designed for your charitable objectives. A "charitable remainder trust" provides a number of benefits for those who wish to pass some of their assets on to charity. The assets that you place into a charitable trust, usually appreciated stocks or other investments, can provide a tax deduction without paying tax on the gain. With a charitable remainder trust, you can stipulate that you receive payments from the trust either as a set annuity or a percentage of the value of the assets. When you die, the entire trust—including the income—will go to the charity.

Explore the different types of trusts and trust provisions that can help you create an estate plan that's just right for you. While estate planning can be complicated, your attorney can guide you through the process to see that your final wishes are carried out.

the ESSENTIALS

1 If you have a family, drawing up a will is vital, in part, because it gives you the opportunity to name the legal guardian for your children.

2 A will also gives you the opportunity to determine how and to whom your assets are distributed.

3 Whenever you have a major change in your life, such as getting married or divorced, take the opportunity to review your accounts and legal documents to ensure their accuracy.

4 A trust can help you to keep your assets out of the probate process. Consult your attorney to determine if a trust is right for you.

5 Preplanning for your funeral, burial, and the disposition of your assets can help to reduce the financial strain on your spouse, dependents, and heirs.

13 [MONEY MATTERS:

Frequently Asked Personal

Finance Questions and Answers]

"Even if you are on the right track, you will still get run over
  if you just sit there."

—Will Rogers

Annuities

Q. **I'm inheriting an annuity from my husband. How will I receive that money?**

A. Depending upon the policy, you may be able to:

1. Leave it intact and thus extend the period of time during which it can continue to grow without triggering taxes.
2. Take it in one lump sum, in which case you'll immediately owe tax on all of the earnings.
3. Annuitize—that is, begin receiving regular payments, giving you a fixed stream of income over a certain number of years or your lifetime. The earnings portion will be taxed as received.

Q. **What does SPDA mean on my annuity contract?**

A. It stands for single premium deferred annuity. You make one lump-sum premium payment and then the annuity grows tax-deferred until you start receiving income.

Q. **My wife has been told she can have a tax-sheltered annuity (TSA) with her new job. What is it?**

A. It's a retirement plan for employees of schools and certain nonprofit organizations. The money is invested in a TSA and contributions, usually through a salary reduction plan, are excluded from gross income. Taxes are not due until withdrawals are made.

Banking

Q. **I have my IRA at my bank. Is it insured?**

A. Yes, if it is at an FDIC-insured bank, it is insured for up to $100,000. IRAs are insured separately from non-retirement accounts—that is, from savings accounts and certificates of deposit. To find out more about bank insurance, log on to www.fdic.gov and then click on "Are My Deposits Insured?" and read the FAQs section.

Q. **Should I put my will in my bank safe deposit box?**

A. Do this only if you also keep signed copies at home and with your lawyer. In some states, contents of the box are sealed upon an owner's death. Then, family members must file court papers to gain access, which can take thirty to forty-five days. Don't store your safe deposit keys in an envelope labeled with the box number, name of the bank, and your name. If the keys fall into the wrong hands, it could be disastrous.

Q. **Why wouldn't my ATM card work in some places in Europe?**

A. Not all foreign banks use our system. Before leaving home next time, ask your bank for a list of ATM locations at your destination.

Bonds

Q. What is the difference between a stock and a bond?

A. A stock is an equity investment. When you buy a stock, you have an ownership share in that corporation. Investors purchase a stock because they either expect it to go up in price and/or because the company pays shareholders a dividend. The price of the stock moves up or down based on how much investors are willing to pay for it.

A bond, on the other hand, is an IOU, a debt instrument. When you purchase a bond you are lending money to the issuer—a corporation, the U.S. Treasury, or a municipality. The issuer must pay back the principal at a particular time, known as the "maturity date." Until the bond matures, you generally receive regular interest payments on your money.

Bonds are generally a more conservative investment, selected for their steady stream of income, while stocks are riskier but offer the potential of greater price appreciation.

Q. We were told that zero coupon bonds are a good way to pay for college. What exactly are they?

A. Years ago, bonds were sold with coupons attached and every six months the bondholder would clip the coupon and take it to a bank to receive the interest payment. Today the interest is automatically mailed to you or deposited into your account. However, the term coupon survives, and as the name implies, a zero coupon bond has no coupon and pays no annual interest.

To compensate, zero coupon bonds are sold at a deep discount from their face value—the amount the bond will be worth when it comes due. For example, 10-year zero coupon bond with a face value of $1,000 may cost only $500 to purchase. The bondholder will receive $1,000 at the time of maturity—in this case, in ten years. Consult with your tax professional to determine all of the the tax consequences before purchasing zero coupon bonds.

Q. I purchased a number of EE savings bonds before I got married. Do I need to have the bonds reissued in my married name?

A. No. When you cash in your bonds, you will be asked to sign your maiden and married names on the bond. Your signature should appear as "Jane H. Doe, changed by marriage to Jane Smith." It's a good idea to have identification with you when cash in the bonds.

Q. My bank told me they couldn't figure out how much my savings bonds are worth. Who can?

A. Go to www.savingsbonds.gov for a free government calculator. Remember, the best time to sell a savings bond is right after the interest is posted. All U.S. savings bonds, including I-bonds, issued on or after May 1997 accrue interest monthly.

College Planning

Q. Should we put money for college in our child's name?

A. Not if you think you will be applying for financial aid. Most colleges use a financial aid formula that requires parents to contribute 5.6 percent of their assets per year (while their child is in college) toward tuition. The child, on the other hand, is required to contribute 35 percent of his or her assets.

Q. We have a Coverdell education savings account (ESA) for our son, but it looks like he may go into the armed forces rather than to college. What will happen to that money?

A. Your son has until he turns thirty to use the money on a tax-free basis. After that, the money can still be withdrawn, but taxes and penalties will be assessed on the income earned by the account. Two other options: 1) the money could be used now for his qualified elementary or secondary education expenses, or 2) it could be transferred to a sibling.

Credit

Q. Our son is going to be a college freshman. We don't want him to have a credit card, yet we know he may need one for airline tickets and emergencies. What should we do?

A. A secured credit card is a good way for your son to learn how to handle credit. After making a deposit in a bank savings account or CD (generally equal to the amount of credit line granted), the bank will issue a credit card. Your son must make timely monthly payments; otherwise the bank can tap into the deposit to cover the amount due. Shop around for the best terms.

Q. I received a letter from my credit card company saying they were shortening the grace period. What does that mean?

A. The grace period, also known as the interest-free period, is the time between the closing date of the billing cycle and the date that you must pay the bill. During this time—generally twenty to thirty days—no interest is charged. Make every effort to pay your bill on time; otherwise, the grace period has no benefit. If your check is delayed in the mail, you can be charged interest, so mail it in plenty of time.

Estate Planning

Q. Is a Roth IRA better than a traditional IRA for leaving money to my family?

A. Yes. With a Roth IRA, you are not required to take out money during your lifetime, so your account can keep on growing tax-free. A traditional IRA, on the other hand, requires you to take taxable withdrawals beginning in the year in which you turn seventy and a half. In addition, you can keep contributing to a Roth as long as you have earned income, which also helps boost the value of the account. Finally, your beneficiary will receive the Roth assets free of federal income tax, whereas in most cases, assets in a traditional IRA are subject to income taxes.

Q. **My wife and I are trying to decide whether to put our home in joint tenancy with the right of survivorship or joint tenancy in common. Which is better?**

A. With joint tenancy with the right of survivorship; the home will pass to the surviving owner without going through probate. Tenancy in common means that you and your spouse each own 50 percent of the home and when one of you dies, that person's share will be owned by whomever the deceased has named in his or her will. It would not necessarily go to the spouse, unless the spouse was so named.

Getting Started

Q. **How can I learn about the stock market?**

A. Begin by reading the financial section of your Sunday newspaper. Then, read one or two popular monthly financial magazines and watch the market news on evening television or listen to a public radio broadcast.

Finally, sign up for an investing course at your local library or school of continuing education.

Q. **Where can I invest a small amount of money in stocks?**

A. A growing number of companies allow investors to buy their first share directly from the company without a fee. Hundreds of others offer this service for a small fee. To find out if the company you are interested in offers this service, log on to the company's Web site or call its investor relations division.

Home Buying

Q. **I am a single woman trying to buy a home. Can I use my IRA?**

A. You can withdraw up to $10,000 from an IRA to finance a first-time home purchase without incurring the 10 percent tax penalty for early withdrawals. However, distribution of any pre-tax earnings from a traditional IRA will be taxed as ordinary income.

You can take advantage of this tax break only if you had no ownership interest in a principal residence during the two-year period ending on the date on which you buy the new home.

Q. **As a veteran, do I get any breaks when purchasing a home?**

A. You may qualify for a low-cost loan if you were on active duty ninety consecutive days during wartime, one hundred eighty-one days during peacetime, or spent six years in the Reserves or National Guard. An often overlooked benefit: An unmarried surviving spouse of a veteran who died on active duty or as the result of a service-connected disability is also eligible for a VA home loan. Some vets are entitled to borrow up to $240,000 with no down payment. Call your local VA office or log on to www.va.gov for more information.

Q. What are points?

A. Points are up-front fees paid to your lender when you close on your mortgage. They are actually figured in percentages—one point is equal to 1 percent of the total loan amount. A one-point fee on a $100,000 mortgage is $1,000; 1.5 points will cost you $1,500. When comparing mortgage rates, say 6.45 percent and 7 percent, you need to know how many points both lenders are charging. The lower rate may not always be better if you have to pay more points.

Insurance

Q. Our travel agent told us we should consider buying an unbundled policy before our next trip because my husband is not well. What should we do?

A. An unbundled policy insures a specific aspect of a trip. For example, some insurers sell an airline ticket protector which covers a nonrefundable airline ticket if you cannot make the flight.

Q. What is a waiver of premium rider on an insurance policy?

A. It means that the insurance company will keep the policy in force if you become disabled and you will not be required to pay any additional premiums. Before purchasing, find out how much it will cost and how the insurance company defines disabled—do you have to be totally disabled or will payments kick in if you're partially disabled? You also want to know if it covers you for life, only until you recover, or for a certain number of years.

Q. I'm thinking of buying term life insurance. How much can I save on my premiums because I do not smoke?

A. It varies from company to company, but can be anywhere from 30 percent to 50 percent. You'll find it pays to shop around to get the best deal.

Investing

Q. Is there any investment that is "risk-free"?

A. No. Every investment has some type of risk, even if it is a small risk. For example, with an FDIC-insured CD, even though your principal and interest is insured by the U.S. government, it has the risk that, after inflation and taxes, you can lose money in terms of purchasing power. And of course, any investment that fluctuates in value can go down.

Q. **I've heard that dollar-cost averaging is a sound strategy. How does it work?**

A. When you dollar-cost average, you invest a specific dollar amount in a fund or stock at regular intervals, say $100 at the beginning of every month. When prices are down, you wind up buying more shares and when prices are high, you buy fewer shares. It's also a low-stress technique—you're not trying to predict the market's movement on a minute-by-minute or day-by-day basis.

Q. **What exactly is insider trading?**

A. Insider trading refers to people who use inside (i.e., nonpublic) information on which to base their decision to buy or sell a company's stock. This typically applies to transactions by people who have confidential information because they work for the company. People who are tipped off by an insider—such as a friend, business associate, or family member—can also be prosecuted—if they trade the stock after receiving nonpublic information.

Q. **How much will it cost me to buy Treasury bonds?**

A. If you purchase them from the government through the Treasury Direct program, there is no fee. For details and a free copy of the *Treasury Direct Investor Kit*, call 800-722-2678 or log on to www.publicdebt.treas.gov. The minimum investment is $1,000 with $1,000 increments. Brokerage firms and banks charge varying fees.

Money & Children

Q. **Can our children own stock?**

A. Not directly, unless they have reached the age of majority, which is usually age eighteen or twenty-one, depending upon the state in which you live. Parents, however, can set up a Uniform Gift to Minors Account (UGMA) with a brokerage firm or mutual fund company to hold stocks or fund shares. Although the account will be in the child's name, the custodian (which could be you) has control of the investment until it comes under the child's control at age eighteen or twenty-one.

Q. **Can children attending college have IRAs?**

A. Yes. If they have earned income, they can put up to $3,000 a year into an IRA—provided they earned that much. If they spent it all on pizza and CDs, you can give them the money to fund the account, but they cannot invest more than the amount they earned in the IRA.

Mortgages

Q. **Does our mother qualify for a reverse mortgage? She is sixty-five.**

A. Yes, she probably does. Generally, homeowners must be sixty-two, occupy the home as a principal residence and have no mortgage (or only one or two payments left). This type of mortgage enables senior citizens who are strapped for cash to borrow against the value of their home. The loan can be paid out in a lump sum, monthly, or set up as a line of credit and tapped as needed. The amount available depends on the age, value, and location of the home. Your mother would need to continue to pay property taxes and insurance and make repairs to maintain the value of the property.

Q. **How much do you save with a 15-year mortgage compared to a 30-year mortgage?**

A. Generally, you'll pay a little less than half the total interest cost of the traditional 30-year fixed-rate mortgage, plus you wind up owning your home in half the time. Lenders usually offer a 15-year mortgage at a slightly lower interest rate than the 30-year. The disadvantage: Monthly payments are 10 to 15 percent higher than with a 30-year mortgage.

Mutual Funds

Q. **How are closed-end funds different from regular funds?**

A. Both open- and closed-end funds invest in portfolios of stocks and/or bonds designed to meet the fund's stated investment goal. Open-end funds continually issue new shares as people invest, and buy back shares when investors sell. Closed-end funds, on the other hand, raise their initial capital by selling a fixed number of shares. Afterwards, the fund is closed and its shares then trade publicly on an exchange, fluctuating in price. Investors usually buy and sell closed-end shares through a stockbroker.

Q. **What is a load fund?**

A. One that has a "load," or sales commission. This commission is deducted from your initial investment and paid to the stockbroker or financial advisor who sold you the fund. For example, if you invest $10,000 in a fund with a front-end load of 8.5 percent, $850 is immediately deducted from your purchase and only $9,150 is invested. Some funds impose a back-end load when you sell.

Q. **I want to invest overseas. What's the difference between a global and an international fund?**

A. Global funds, also called world funds, invest in U.S. stocks and bonds, as well as those of other countries. International funds, on the other hand, invest exclusively in stocks or bonds outside the United States. There's yet another type of foreign fund—regional funds, which focus on geographic areas, such as Europe, the Pacific rim, or Latin America.

Retirement Planning

Q. **We are selling our home and moving to a retirement community. In order to take advantage of the capital gains tax exclusion, we have to prove that it was our primary residence. How do we do that?**

A. The key qualifiers are that the home you are selling is where 1) you are registered to vote; 2) your driver's license is issued; 3) you file your state income tax return; 4) you receive most of your mail, including bank and brokerage account and credit card statements; and 5) you maintain memberships in social clubs, a place of worship, etc.

Q. **What is the difference between a Roth IRA and a traditional IRA?**

A. With a traditional IRA (if you qualify), you can often deduct the money you contribute to the IRA, but you pay taxes on the money when you withdraw it during retirement. With a Roth IRA, you can't deduct the money you contribute, but you pay no taxes on the money you withdraw after you're retired or for other qualified purposes.

Q. **Can I put extra money into my IRA? I want to try to build up the account while I'm still working.**

A. Whether you intentionally or accidentally contribute too much to your IRA, the excess amount is subject to a 6 percent excise tax. The tax continues, year after year, as long as the excess remains in the account. Consult your tax professional; in most cases, if you take out the excess money on or before the date your tax return is due, no excise tax will be charged. The income earned on these extra funds, which also must be taken out, will be taxed as ordinary income and is subject to the penalty on early distributions.

Safe Investments

Q. **What are some really safe investments for small amounts of money?**

A. If you want to be able to tap into your money at any time, consider an FDIC-insured bank savings account or a bank money market account. Both are insured up to $100,000, but their yields are low. Money market funds (offered by mutual funds), pay slightly higher yields and, although they are not FDIC-insured, they are generally safe. If you don't need immediate access to your money, you'll get higher rates with an FDIC-insured bank certificate of deposit. Generally, the longer you tie up your money, the higher the rate—a 5-year CD will usually have a higher yield than a 1-year CD.

Q. **What are the differences between I-bonds and EE savings bonds?**

A. The differences primarily involve how interest rates are figured and their purchase prices. EE bonds sell at a 50 percent discount from face value—a $50 bond actually costs just $25. Interest is based on 90 percent of the average yield on 5-year Treasury securities for the preceding six months and compounds tax-deferred until the bonds are redeemed or reach maturity. There are no state or local taxes and no federal taxes for qualified investors who use the bond proceeds to pay for qualified college costs. I-bonds, or inflation bonds, are issued at face value—a $50 bond costs $50. Interest compounds tax-deferred until the bond is redeemed and is figured on 1) a fixed rate determined at the time of purchase remains the same for the life of the bond, and 2) a semiannual rate adjusted for inflation. Both of these I-bond rates are combined to determine the rate for the next six months. Rates for EE and I-bonds change on November 1 and May 1. Details: 800-US-BONDS or www.savingsbonds.gov.

Saving

Q. **What's the best way to save?**

A. It depends upon your particular spending habits, but give these five ways a try:

- **Pay yourself first by making savings your first check.** The dollar amount is less important than the habit.

- **Sign up for automatic savings plans.** Arrange for a certain amount to be taken out of your paycheck and automatically put in your savings or money market fund.

- **Leave credit cards at home.** Pay with cash or by check. (Carry several traveler's checks for emergencies.)

- **Keep making payments.** When you've paid off your student loan, car loan, or mortgage, continue to write a check for the same amount (or at least half the amount) every month and put it into savings.

- **Save change (better yet, dollar bills) at the end of the day.** Small amounts add up quickly. Once a week, empty your piggy bank into your savings account.

Stocks

Q. **I'm always hearing that the Dow is up or down. What does that really mean? What's in the Dow?**

A. The Dow Jones Industrial Average is the most popular indicator of the overall, day-to-day direction of the stock market. It consists of thirty large "blue-chip" stocks that are leaders in their industries and are widely held by both individual and institutional investors. The average is arrived at each trading day by adding up the prices of these thirty key stocks and then dividing the total price by a divisor. The thirty stocks that make up this influential index are selected by editors at *The Wall Street Journal*.

Q. **I bought a stock that pays a dividend but my broker says I won't be receiving it. How can that be?**

A. You purchased a stock that is "ex-dividend"—without a dividend. A company's board of directors meets each quarter to decide how much (if any) will be paid to shareholders as a dividend. If they declare a dividend, they then set a "record date." Had you owned the stock on or before the "record date" you would have been entitled to the dividend. (When a stock trades ex-dividend, the symbol "x" appears next to its listing in the newspaper.)

Q. **Why do some of my stocks pay dividends and others do not?**

A. Companies are not required to pay dividends. In fact, small, fast-growing companies usually decide to reinvest profits back into the company to help it grow. Well-established companies, on the other hand, often elect to return a portion of earnings to shareholders in the form of a dividend. If business is off, it is not uncommon for a company to reduce or even eliminate dividends. On the other hand, if business is booming, the company may decide to increase dividends. An increase is usually an indication that the corporation is confident about its future.

Q. **How do you figure out a stock's yield?**

A. Take the dollar value of a stock's annual dividend and divide it by the share price. For example, if a $20 stock pays $1 a year in dividends, its yield is 5 percent. Even if the stock doesn't go up in price, you still earn a 5 percent annual return from the dividend.

Taxes

Q. **I did a lot of volunteer work last year. What can I deduct?**

A. If you itemize, you can deduct: 1) the actual cost for oil and gas used driving to and from a volunteer site (or take the standard IRS deduction of 14 cents/mile), 2) tolls, 3) parking fees, and 4) meals and lodging if your volunteer work required you to be away overnight. If you were required to wear a uniform, the purchase and cleaning costs are deductible. However, the uniform cannot be suitable for any other purpose—a Red Cross uniform will pass muster with the IRS, but T-shirts and jeans will not. The cost of materials and supplies you purchase as part of your volunteer activity is also deductible.

Q. **Can I deduct my IRA contribution?**

A. It depends. Contributions to a Roth IRA are never deductible. However, you can deduct your full contribution to a traditional IRA if you are not covered by a retirement plan at work. If you have an employer-sponsored plan and your income is over a certain amount (which is periodically adjusted), your deduction will be reduced or eliminated.

Now, Get Ready to Make the Most of Your Personal Finances

Congratulations! You've finished reading the *H&R Block Personal Finance Advisor*. You should now know a great deal more about how to make your hard-earned money work even harder for you. You can begin the journey toward realizing your own personal finance goals and dreams by taking the fundamentals covered in these pages and applying them to your own financial situation.

Remember, you don't have to travel alone when planning your personal finances. You may want to work with a financial advisor on some of the tougher financial issues you face and for assistance when putting together your financial plan. The more knowledge you have of personal finance and your own personal situation, the more an advisor can help you with the decisions you have to make.

And don't forget about your online learning resource, hrblock.com/advisor. This resource will enable you to access a variety of interactive tools and calculators to help you set and work toward achieving your financial goals.

Hopefully, this book has helped you learn how to map out a route to your financial goals. As you travel toward your destination, there will certainly be navigational adjustments you will need to make. Regardless of the detours, remember to stay focused on your goals. Happy financial planning!

resources

Banking and Credit Unions

For information about banks, credit unions, insured deposits, how to select and use checking accounts, and much more, contact:

- aboutchecking.com
  www.aboutchecking.com

- American Bankers Association
  www.aba.com

- Credit Union National Association
  www.cuna.org

- Federal Deposit Insurance Corporation
  www.fdic.gov

- National Credit Union Administration
  www.ncua.gov

College Planning

To learn more about planning for college, including selecting and applying for admission to a college, saving for college, financial aid, and much more, contact:

- The College Board
  www.collegeboard.com

- College Savings Plan Network
  www.collegesavings.org or 877-277-6496

- Free Application for Federal Student Aid (FAFSA)
  www.fafsa.ed.gov or 800-4-FED-AID
  (800-433-3243)

- Sallie Mae loans
  www.salliemae.com or 888-2-SALLIE
  (888-272-5543)

- U.S. Department of Education
  www.ed.gov

Credit Counseling

For information about low-cost or no-cost organizations that may be able to help you rebuild your credit or get out of debt, contact:

- National Foundation for Credit Counseling (NFCC)
  www.nfcc.org

- Federal Trade Commission (FTC)
  www.ftc.gov

Credit Reports

To order a copy of your credit report, report fraud, or correct an error, contact one of the three credit reporting services:

- Equifax
  www.equifax.com or 800-685-1111

- experian
  www.experian.com or 888-397-3742

- TransUnion
  www.transunion.com or 800-888-4213

Credit Scores

To find how credit scoring works, what your score is, and tips on improving it contact:

- Fair, Isaac
  www.myfico.com

Estate Planning

For information about estate planning contact:

- AARP
  www.aarp.org

- American Bar Association
  www.abanet.org

Homes and Mortgages

To obtain more information about buying and selling homes, the value of home ownership, how to select a mortgage lender, and various financing options, contact:

- Fannie Mae loans
  www.fanniemae.com
- Freddie Mac loans
  www.freddiemac.com
- Ginnie Mae loans
  www.ginniemae.gov
- National Association of Realtors®
  www.realtor.com
- U.S. Department of Housing and Urban Development (HUD)
  www.hud.gov
- U.S. Department of Veterans Affairs (VA)
  www.va.gov

H&R Block can provide you with comprehensive information on home mortgages, including first-time home buying, refinancing, home equity loans, and debt consolidation. You can also find educational information and many useful tools and calculators to help you make informed home ownership-related decisions.

- H&R Block
  www.hrblock.com or 877-HRBLOCK (877-472-5625)

Insurance

To learn more about all types of insurance, including a variety of products and services, how to compare policies, and about the companies that issue the polices, contact:

- A.M. Best Company
  www.ambest.com
- Insurance Information Institute
  www.iii.org

- Medicare
  www.medicare.gov
- National Association of Insurance Commissioners
  www.naic.org

Investing Education

There are a variety of sources for learning more about investing, including:

- Alliance for Investor Education
  www.investoreducation.org
- American Association of Individual Investors
  www.aaii.com
- Barron's
  www.barrons.com
- Bloomberg
  www.bloomberg.com
- Brill Editorial Services Inc.
  www.fundsinteractive.com
- Forbes
  www.forbes.com
- INVESTools.com
  www.investools.com
- Investor's Business Daily
  www.investors.com
- Morningstar.com
  www.morningstar.com
- National Association of Investors Corporation
  www.better-investing.org
- National Association of Securities Dealers
  www.nasd.com
- Standard & Poor's
  www.standardandpoors.com
- The Wall Street Journal
  www.wsj.com
- Value Line
  www.valueline.com
- H&R Block
  www.hrblock.com or 800-HRBLOCK (800-472-5625)

Miscellaneous Consumer Information

Information on a variety of topics from government benefits and assistance to money matters, healthcare, and identity theft can be obtained from the federal government. Contact:

- **FirstGov**
  www.consumer.gov
- **GovBenefits**
  www.govbenefits.gov

Personal Finance

To access educational programs and financial tools for people of all ages, contact:

- **Employee Benefit Research Institute**
  www.choosetosave.org

H&R Block can provide you with a wide range of personal finance information. Understand the tax and financial aspects of major life events, use online resources and tools to see how fast your savings can grow, prepare your taxes online, get your, tax questions answered, learn the basics of investing, get quotes, invest online, pre-qualify for a mortgage, plus much more.

- **H&R Block**
  www.hrblock.com or 800-HRBLOCK (800-472-5625)

Retirement Planning

Contact the Social Security Administration to request an estimate of what you'll receive from Social Security, or request a copy of Form SSA-7004.

- **Social Security Administration**
  www.ssa.gov or 800-772-1213

For information about profit sharing and 401(k) plans contact:

- **Profit Sharing Council of America**
  www.401k.org

H&R Block can assist you with your plans for retirement. Visit our web site for information and tips on planning for retirement. Access a variety of interactive calculators and tools to help you estimate how big a nest egg you might need for retirement and to see how quickly your savings can multiply.

- **H&R Block**
  www.hrblock.com or 800-HRBLOCK (800-472-5625)

Savings Bonds

For information about investing in savings bonds, contact:

- **Bureau of the Public Debt**
  www.savingsbonds.gov

Taxes

For a variety of resource material including forms, publications, advice, and tax-related tools, contact:

- **Internal Revenue Service (IRS)**
  www.irs.gov or 800-829-1040

H&R Block has a wide selection of available resources for you. These include tax preparation and filing options, forms, advice, planning tools, tax preparation courses, and much more. To find out more, visit the retail location nearest you, or:

- **H&R Block**
  www.hrblock.com, or 800-HRBLOCK (800-472-5625)

index

about H&R Block

H&R Block, Inc. (www.hrblock.com) is a diversified company with subsidiaries that deliver tax services and financial advice, investment and mortgage products and services, and business accounting and consulting services.

As the world's largest tax services company, H&R Block served nearly 23 million clients during fiscal year 2002. Clients were served at H&R Block's approximately 10,400 retail offices worldwide with its award-winning software, TaxCut®, and through its online tax services.

Investment services and securities products are offered through H&R Block Financial Advisors, Inc., member NYSE, SIPC. H&R Block, Inc. and H&R Block Services, Inc. are not registered broker-dealers. H&R Block Mortgage Corp. offers retail mortgage products. Option One Mortgage Corp. offers wholesale mortgage products and a wide range of mortgage services. RSM McGladrey, Inc. serves mid-sized businesses with accounting, tax, and consulting services.

Call **H&R Block Mortgage** today to get a

free, no obligation

Custom Mortgage Analysis.

At H&R Block Mortgage, our goal is to make sure you find the loan or refinance option that's appropriate for your specific needs. We have a variety of loan products, so you may qualify to:

- Refinance your mortgage and lower your monthly payments
- Consolidate other debts into one simple loan payment
- Make home improvements
- Borrow money for college tuition
- Get cash out

Call now at **1-877-HRBLOCK**
It just takes a few minutes.

H&R BLOCK®
mortgage

Get a **free** financial review and a **good night's sleep**.

Whether you're saving for a new home, higher education, or a much-needed vacation, our experienced financial advisors will help you plan your financial future so you can rest easy.

To schedule your appointment at an H&R Block office near you, call 1-800-HRBLOCK (select the Financial and Investment Services option) today.

Call **1-800-HRBLOCK** today and get a free Financial Review.

H&R BLOCK®
financial advisors

WE HELPED PEOPLE WHO OVERPAID GET BACK AN AVERAGE OF $1,300.

CAN YOU SAY "CHA-CHING"

Take the FREE Double Check Challenge at H&R Block

Thousands of Americans overpaid nearly $1 billion in taxes last year. Did you overpay? H&R Block will double check your past years' returns to see if you're entitled to more money back.

Those who overpaid and refiled with us got an average of $1,300 back. Have us double-check your previous years' tax returns free to see if we can find you more. And, we can help you re-file* past returns so you can get back the money you deserve.

See reverse side for more details.

H&R BLOCK®

just plain smart™

find money
you didn't even
know you'd lost.

Double Check Challenge

Americans overpay nearly $1 billion in taxes each year.
Is some of it yours?

How it Works

1. Bring copies of your past returns to an H&R Block office.

2. Our H&R Block professionals will review up to three years of past returns - at no cost to you.

3. If we discover an error, we can help you re-file past returns so you can get back the money you deserve (re-filing fees apply).

Benefits

Found money - Clients who overpaid and re-filed with us received an average of $1,300 back.

Join the long list of clients who took—and benefited from—the Double Check Challenge

H&R BLOCK®